Women
World Leaders

■■

Women
World Leaders

Fifteen great politicians tell their stories

LAURA A. LISWOOD

An Imprint of HarperCollins*Publishers*

Pandora
An Imprint of HarperCollins*Publishers*
77–85 Fulham Palace Road,
Hammersmith, London W6 8JB
1160 Battery Street,
San Francisco, California 94111–1213

First published in hardback by Pandora 1995
This paperback edition 1996
1 3 5 7 9 10 8 6 4 2

Laura A. Liswood asserts the moral right to
be identified as the author of this work

A catalogue record for this book is available from the British Library

ISBN 0 04 440905 2

Printed and bound in Great Britain by
Caledonian International Book Manufacturing Ltd, Glasgow

*There is no democracy in our
beautifully democratic countries.
Why? Women have not the same part
in decision making as men have.*

VIGDIS FINNBOGADÓTTIR,
President of Iceland

*We are not yet there, but it's
very important that we see that
more and more countries are appointing
women as their political leaders, as
prime ministers, as presidents, and
I think that's a very important
development.*

MARIA LIBERIA-PETERS,
**Former Prime Minister,
Netherlands Antilles**

Contents

■■

Acknowledgements

It is impossible to list all of the wonderful, supportive individuals who helped make this project possible. Many were government employees. United States Information Agency cultural affairs officers, US State Department country desk officers, US embassy personnel – including ambassadors and their staffs who guided me – all provided crucial information, listened with interest and kept me company. The DC office of Senator Ted Kennedy kindly contacted the embassies of Pakistan and Bangladesh on my behalf. Overseas, many people in the countries I visited helped to ensure that interviews occurred and were always friendly, no matter how busy.

I want to thank UNIFEM, a division of the United Nations which deals with women's and children's issues, and the Kongsgaard Foundation for their initial financial assistance. Also, my grateful thanks to Adrienne Arsht Feldman for her continual wise counsel; to Dr Christine di Stefano of the University of Washington, Seattle, for my political science education; and to Laura Boydston, for working so tirelessly. Patricia Coburn was an essential part of this undertaking. My thanks also to Kristina Veirs for research assistance and word processing of the manuscript.

Editors always deserve to be recognized: Belinda Budge, Sara Dunn and Karen Holden of Pandora, and Rebecca Lewis, of HarperCollins, certainly do. My thanks to Dana for being on the other end of the long-distance telephone calls so many times. Finally, to friends and family around the world who believe in women as leaders – my warm appreciation.

Introduction

■■

This book – one aspect of the Women's Leadership Project – is the result of many fascinating journeys. The interviews with women prime ministers and presidents of the world on which the book is based carried me to countries as disparate as Iceland and Sri Lanka, Ireland and Bangladesh, Poland and the Philippines.

Questions had been forming in my mind for some time regarding women and governance – I had read essays by feminists and political scientists about why more women should be in politics. When women – one half of the world – are as severely underrepresented in governing, across the world, as they currently are, something is very wrong. Why, I asked myself, are qualities that we often identify as feminine – qualities of nurturing and cooperating, among others – not more active ingredients in world politics? And how could I get actual proof that women's leadership makes a difference?

One day in late 1992 I read a short study published by the Center for the American Woman and Politics (CAWP) located at Rutgers University. It was a survey, carried out by Debra Dodson, of women elected to state legislatures. 'Women are diverse and some are more likely than others to reshape the policy agenda and work on women's rights bills,' noted Dodson, 'but it is clear that, overall, women lawmakers do more to help women than their male colleagues.' The survey showed that women *do* reshape the policy agenda through their legislative priorities and their work on women's rights bills.

It also provided evidence that women public officials are changing the way government works. The women legislators were more likely than men to bring citizens into the political process, to favour government in public view rather than government behind closed doors, and to be responsive to groups previously denied full access to the policy-making process.

No matter that the study was narrowly focused on state legislators. It was the first quantitative research I had seen that went beyond general ideas of the need for gender balance and greater roles for women in politics. My MBA 'need for statistical proof' was satisfied; there was a difference, and it was not merely academic theory that said so.

I was in my studio overlooking Elliott Bay in Seattle, Washington, and that year I had co-founded a group called May's List in Washington State. We wanted to emulate the highly successful national model of EMILY's LIST – to bring power fundraising for women candidates to the local level and 'bundle checks' for women running for city council or mayor or state representative. We understood that we had to 'fill the pipeline' – to help women run at all levels – if we were to have more women leaders. EMILY's LIST – 'Early Money Is Like Yeast; it makes the dough rise' – grew out of the recognized difficulty women running for office had in raising the initial money for campaigns. In politics money begets money, which Ellen Malcolm, Founder of EMILY's LIST, realized; she did something to overcome that barrier.

So I was primed and delighted to read the CAWP report. As I watched the ferries float by on the bay, I thought: How can I find out what it is like, this women's leadership? Where are women exercising power at the very top?

I cannot say I saw my many journeys opening out before me at that moment. No. But I was beginning to wonder how I could ask those who were in power what it was like. I was thinking about something else as well. I wanted to go to the Fourth World Conference on Women, to be sponsored by the United Nations in Beijing in September, 1995. I knew little about it, but in another example of how 'you find what you need when you are ready to learn it,' I read in *Ms* magazine in 1993 that a Mrs Gertrude Mongella of Tanzania had been appointed by UN Secretary-General Boutros Boutros-Ghali to be the Secretary-General of the Fourth World Conference. So I called. And wrote. And got an appointment with her. (Thanks to two supportive UN secretaries, Elizabeth Ellers and Juliet Kiswaga, who helped make it happen!)

I proposed the idea of a video of various women world leaders to be shown at the conference. Would Mrs Mongella support that? Neither of us quite knowing what 'that' meant. She said 'Yes, why not?'

Using that slim but crucial bridge, I approached Madame Corazon Aquino through the help of old friends and new friends. She said, yes, she would meet me. Such excitement, such amazement! The fax from her came on a Friday. What was I to do? I rushed and called and faxed. My luck held as an under-secretary of tourism, Ms Mina Gabor, graciously offered to arrange for the camera crew to be there and would also be there herself to support my effort. A *Seattle Times* reporter, Eric Nalder, suggested interview techniques.

I was so busy that there was little time for self-doubt. I wanted to know about leaders' styles, about family backgrounds and values, about how women did their jobs. Was the public's expectation of them different than for men? Let them talk of power; let them just talk!

Before I left for the Philippines, I spoke with State Representative Velma Veloria, the first Filipina–American woman elected to Washington state office. She gave me names of college friends. So did others. I was armed with a list of women to meet. And I did meet them. Women who had organized to help other women.

A similar process occurred each time I wanted to approach a woman leader after that. I never expected to meet nearly every living woman president or prime minister who served for at least nine months.[1] I just kept asking. Explaining. Being scrutinized. Who was I with? What purpose did I have? Who would see my video?

I received immense help from US State Department desk officers used to journalists' requests for interviews. They directed me to USIA press officers, whom I would fax. Who would send the request on. In

the meantime I would talk with country-specific Embassy press officers, to further my requests. All were courteous, though not all were
encouraging. Imagine the impossible number of requests each leader
gets! And who was I? Not Kate Adie or Barbara Walters or CNN or
Italian superinterviewer Oriana Fallaci (with whom I once spent a
glorious three hours talking of Golda Meir, Indira Gandhi, and her
own life of 'writing plays' – Ms Fallaci's term for interviewing).
However things were happening; I just stayed at it. Never *demanding*, and thus avoiding getting a complete No. Was I a nuisance?
Probably. But no one said so to me. I was sometimes warned with a
laugh by USIA personnel that, if I got an appointment, the exact time
would come suddenly without warning, and I must just be prepared
to react. Other appointments, I was told, would be given in a more
Nordic style – exact time, length of stay, all very firm. There would
be, as it turned out, long waits in hotels around the world, camera
crews on standby.

I can now say this: Had I known the enormity of my undertaking
in advance, how much knowledge I should have amassed in order to
do it, this project would not have been done by me. In the end, I just
did it. The impossible became the inevitable.

Some comments on the interviews. They were from thirty to seventy
minutes in length. I would have loved more time – but time is something that women ruling at the top have far too little of.

The heart of what I was after was how the responses of women
leaders compared across an issue – both the divergences and similarities of response. To me that would be of most interest. Once the
interviews were on videotape, transcripts were derived and major
themes organized. The Women's Leadership Project has produced
both a film and this book.

I should point out that, since history moves on and politics
changes constantly, some of the women I interviewed may be out of
office when the reader opens this book. A few of the women regularly

move in and out of prime ministerships as the political parties which they head win or lose elections. In 1995 one more woman – Chandrika Bandaranaike Kumaratunga of Sri Lanka – may qualify for inclusion in this book by virtue of being in power for at least nine months.

What struck us? What did we learn? My chapters are organized by theme, and messages will become clear as the reader progresses. But I would note my awe at what some of these women have taken on. Because there have been so few women governing at the top throughout history, all are pathfinders. Role models for them are few, and many have experienced events which it is difficult for most us to imagine upsetting our own lives. And yet even Benazir Bhutto talks of the burdens of being a mother, and Maria Liberia-Peters says her children always want mommy. So they are flesh and blood, as we are. And their numbers will increase. I particularly anticipate the first woman president of my own country, the United States. I hope that by the time the reader finishes this book, it will have become obvious what it takes to bring more women to the top. There are many ways in which the resources necessary can be helped along by every individual.

I think it will be useful to the reader to become acquainted with these women leaders through the brief biographies which make up my first chapter – to flesh out each of the fifteen interviewees in the reader's mind. And study the face in her photograph on the cover, too. In addition, I have tried to provide some sense of the milieu in which each woman must function, in a section on geogender and country backgrounds later on in the book. Obviously, leading a country in which many women are still illiterate is not the same experience as operating in one where standards of education are high, nor is leading a wealthy and stable nation the same as leading a poor country with a history of military takeovers. Many, many factors will make a difference in what a leader – female or male – can hope to achieve. My section on geography and gender tries to introduce some of this necessary background.

It has been a great privilege to be in the company of so many outstanding women. I now know that it is not impossible for a woman to lead a country.

LAURA A. LISWOOD
Seattle, Washington, March, 1995

The following presidents and prime ministers of the world were interviewed for this book:

CORAZON AQUINO, *Former President, The Philippines*

SIRIMAVO BANDARANAIKE, *Former Prime Minister, Sri Lanka*

BENAZIR BHUTTO, *Prime Minister, Pakistan*

GRO HARLEM BRUNDTLAND, *Prime Minister, Norway*

VIOLETA CHAMORRO, *President, Nicaragua*

EUGENIA CHARLES, *Prime Minister, Dominica*

TANSU CILLER, *Prime Minister, Turkey*

EDITH CRESSON, *Former Prime Minister, France*

VIGDIS FINNBOGADÓTTIR, *President, Iceland*

MARIA LIBERIA-PETERS, *Former Prime Minister, Netherlands Antilles*

KAZIMIERA PRUNSKIENE, *Former Prime Minister, Lithuania*

MARY ROBINSON, *President, Ireland*

HANNA SUCHOCKA, *Former Prime Minister, Poland*

MARGARET THATCHER, *Former Prime Minister, Great Britain*

KHALEDA ZIA, *Prime Minister, Bangladesh*

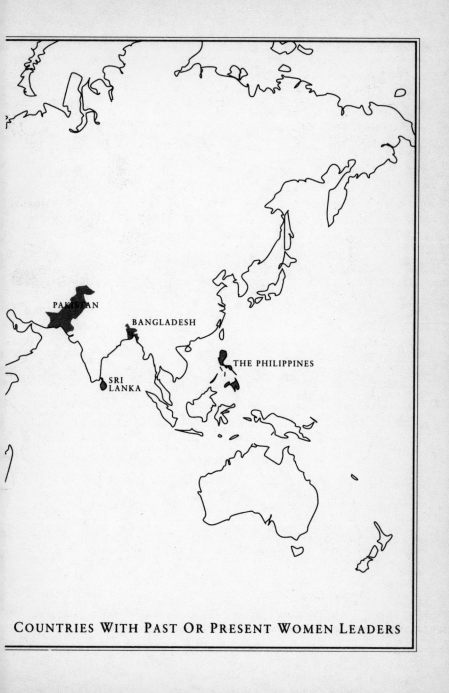

COUNTRIES WITH PAST OR PRESENT WOMEN LEADERS

CHAPTER 1

Biographies

CORAZON AQUINO
Former President, The Philippines

Manila – where I flew to meet former president Corazon Aquino – was troubled with blackouts, traffic jams and pickpockets. Security guards and metal detectors were at the ready. Jeepneys with names like BABY and LOVE BOY carried passengers up and down the streets. The headlines of the *Manila Star* read: 'More Terrorist Bombings Warned, Ramos Not Considering Martial Law.'

President Fidel Ramos is the person Aquino favoured as her successor. He took her side in the days of People Power, when thousands of Filipinos came into the streets to support her. When I met with Aquino at her office in Quezon City, on a hot and humid day, she was poised and gracious; she became especially animated when talking of the women's development projects which are now her special interest. Religious images in her office testified to her devout Catholicism.

...not being president anymore, I do not have the kind of resources necessary in order to organize everywhere. But ... I ... go to the affluent women first because I have to tap them and their personal resources ... I feel since they have been blessed, then they're the ones who really should be prepared to make ... extra sacrifices in order to reach out for those who have less in life.

CORAZON AQUINO

Corazon Cojuangco Aquino, president of the Philippines from 1986 until 1992, was born in Tarlac Province, Luzon, on 25 January 1933. Her powerful landowning family – one of the fifty or sixty important families of her country – was politically active: her father was a congressman, both grandfathers were senators.

A devout Catholic, Aquino was educated at Catholic schools in Manila and the United States. She graduated from Mount St Vincent College in New York City and returned to the Philippines to attend law school at Far Eastern University. In 1954, however, she made a decision which was to have more consequences than she or anyone could have imagined: she left law school after her first year to marry Benigno Aquino, Jr., a successful young journalist who would soon leave journalism for politics to become one of his country's martyrs.

Like Corazon, 'Ninoy' Aquino came from a wealthy landowning family involved in sugar plantations; however, an article which he authored for *Foreign Affairs* magazine in 1968 showed his awareness of his country's problems: 'Here is a land in which a few are spectacularly rich while the masses remain abjectly poor ... a land consecrated to democracy but run by an entrenched plutocracy ... honeycombed with graft.' Ferdinand Marcos had come to power in 1965; in 1972 he was to declare martial law and throw Ninoy Aquino into prison for more than seven years.

Corazon Aquino has defined the period of her husband's imprisonment as the pivotal crisis in her life. A shy person who had, until then, devoted herself to a private existence raising five children, she became her husband's link with the outside world, receiving weekly tutoring from him as he tried to remain politically involved from behind prison walls. In time Ninoy was allowed to go to the US for treatment for medical problems. The family settled in Newton, Massachusetts, from 1980 to 1983, with Ninoy a research fellow at Harvard University and MIT, the Massachusetts Institute of Technology. However, when Marcos declared elections for 1984, Benigno Aquino decided to return home. His plane had barely touched down at Manila Airport, on 21 August 1983, when he was assassinated. Word was telephoned to his family, still in the US.

'Cory' Aquino returned to the Philippines to lead processions to her husband's lying-in-state, and to his grave. She began working for anti-Marcos candidates, 56 of whom gained seats in the National Assembly in October of 1985. Although not seen as a political leader immediately upon her return, Aquino was eventually recognized by anti-Marcos politicians as someone who could mobilize the electorate. A 'Cory for President' movement began; she asked for, and received, a million signatures in support of her candidacy within a month. A 45-day election campaign started, with her opponent,

Marcos, occasionally declaring that 'a woman's place is in the bedroom'. When Marcos eventually tried to steal the election, the people of Manila came into the streets by the hundreds of thousands; two of Marcos's key military leaders revolted. Marcos was forced to fly into exile. Corazon Aquino was her country's president.

Aquino saw her mandate as a continuation of her husband's attempt to restore democracy to the Philippines. She called for a new constitution which set more limits on presidential power; she abided by that constitution when she left office after one six-year term. Her presidency was troubled by continual attempted military revolts; seven attempts of varying degrees of gravity resulted in more than 150 deaths. When Aquino made her first official visit to the Philippine Military Academy, she reminded those present: 'This revolution began with a bullet shot by a soldier into the head of my husband.'

In her interview for this book, Aquino spoke of her efforts to initiate military reform: 'Well, first the military found it extremely difficult to accept a woman commander-in-chief. And certainly it was also difficult for me ... I was in fact very directly responsible for putting in ... reforms in ... selecting the colonels who would become the generals. Before my time, the process was very subjective ... the criteria ... had not been quantified.'

Aquino also concerned herself with the appointment of women to high positions. She tapped a number of them to head departments or commissions, and appointed three women (of fifteen justices) to the Supreme Court.

In the later years of her administration, Aquino focused her attention on assisting the development of non-governmental organizations (NGOs) and cooperatives. This is the work she has chosen to continue now that she is out of office. As she once told a Filipina journalist: 'Government cannot do it alone. This is the reason I want to be more involved in the NGOs.'

SIRIMAVO BANDARANAIKE

Former Prime Minister, Sri Lanka

Sirimavo Bandaranaike's hobby is growing roses, and some of these beautiful flowers were on show when I visited her home in November of 1993 to interview her. In the periods of her prime ministerships, she told me, she got little time to garden, little personal time at all.

'Mrs. Banda', as she is known in Sri Lanka, has dark eyes, a skin of light tan and her hair severely pulled back in a bun. A number of male aides stood by during our interview, somewhat on guard, ready to assist her as needed. During the course of the visit, she showed me photographs of her husband, Solomon, and of members of the Gandhi family, with whom they were friends.

––––––––––––

– How do you think that men and women differ as leaders?
– Well, probably women deal with things a little more humanely. Men are tough and impatient.

SIRIMAVO BANDARANAIKE

In 1960, Sirimavo Bandaranaike of Sri Lanka (then Ceylon) became the world's first woman prime minister.

Born 17 April 1916 into a well-off and politically involved family with five children, the former Sirimavo Ratwatte described her upbringing when she was interviewed for this book.

I was brought up in my maternal grandfather's home by my parents and grandparents, who belonged to the landed gentry ... We were a very closely knit family ... We are a Buddhist family and followed Buddhist philosophy.

Bandaranaike was sent to a Catholic convent school in Colombo, where she remained until the age of eighteen. Six years later her parents arranged for her marriage to an Oxford-educated lawyer-politician who also came from a wealthy landowning family. Her new father-in-law had once been a chief aide to the British governor of Ceylon.

By the time of Ceylon's near-complete independence from Britain in 1948 (Ceylon still had a governor-general tie to Britain's Crown), Sirimavo Bandaranaike was raising children – there were eventually three – and was active in the Ceylon Women's Association (Lanka Mahila Samiti). Its aim was 'to ameliorate rural conditions and improve the social and economic life of the people, particularly in the rural areas.' Family planning and women's development became two of her concerns.

Bandaranaike's husband Solomon, meanwhile, had been elected to the new House of Representatives and had served as minister of health and local government in the cabinet of D D Senanayake, Ceylon's first prime minister after independence. A socialist and strong nationalist, Solomon Bandaranaike eventually, in 1956, became prime minister himself. Part of his programme involved replacing English with Sinhalese as the national language, and making Buddhism the national religion. These proposals – opposed by Ceylon's Tamil-speaking Hindu minority – set off riots. Eventually a state of emergency was declared. In September of 1959 Solomon Bandaranaike was assassinated.

His sorrowing widow was asked to campaign on behalf of his party, the Sri Lanka Freedom Party (SLFP). In May of 1960 she became its head. In July the SLFP won 75 of 151 seats in the House of Representatives. 'Mrs Banda', as party leader, was appointed prime minister.

Despite an initial reluctance to play a political role, Sirimavo Bandaranaike did not serve briefly and then retire into private life. She became in time a professional politician, sometimes in and sometimes out of office. A leftist-nationalist like her husband, her politics often challenged the Cold War policies of the United States and were themselves challenged by ultra-leftists within Ceylon. During her second term as prime minister from 1970 to 1977, (the first was from 1960 until 1965), Ceylon became the Socialist Republic of Sri Lanka, with no remaining political ties to Britain.

Bandaranaike ran for president of her country in 1986, but did not win. In 1989 she won a seat in the National Assembly and, at 73 years of age, headed the opposition. In 1994, at the age of 78, she was once again in the news as her party's leader, and in August 1994, after new elections, had the pleasure of seeing her daughter – Chandrika Bandaranaike Kumaratunga, age 48 – take over to become the new prime minister of Sri Lanka, the third prime minister in the family. Chandrika Kumaratunga campaigned on the platform of a free market, a cleaner government and peace negotiations to end the Tamil/Sinhalese civil war, which has taken many thousands of lives since 1983. Kumaratunga heads a multi-party coalition government; she was educated at the Sorbonne.

BENAZIR BHUTTO
Prime Minister, Pakistan

In a dazzlingly bright blue dress with black dots, and with her usual Muslim headscarf over her dark hair, Benazir Bhutto made a bit of a grand entrance as she appeared in the luxurious living room of her home to greet me. She sat down on a beige sofa and interacted tenderly with her shy, very young, daughter. A sealed package of Susan B Anthony coins which I had brought as a gift was opened by Bhutto's security staff – one small sign of the safety measures surrounding her.

Bhutto is dignified, eloquent and charismatic. She speaks English with touches of an Oxbridge accent, thanks to her several years in Britain. She is a fiery public speaker who can animate large crowds of admirers.

I was extremely idealistic as a child; I still am idealistic to a great extent. But I found that in life everything is not up front as we would wish it to be and that some of us are too simple. I think I was a very simple, naive person, and I have learnt that life is not always fair, it is not always just, but even if it is not fair, and even if it is not just, it is important to go on working for what you believe in.

BENAZIR BHUTTO

8

Benazir Bhutto's has been a hard journey in a harsh land. Pakistan's military has governed her country for half of the years since independence from Britain in 1947. As in some other nations – Guatemala comes to mind – parliamentary government in Pakistan masks the power of the generals, who stand ready to intervene in political affairs. They hanged Bhutto's father in 1979 – an event which changed her life.

Benazir Bhutto had just returned from several years of study abroad, in 1977, when the army surrounded her family's house and took her father, the prime minister, away to jail. Zulfikar Bhutto had two sons and two daughters; Benazir was his favourite. In prison, he asked her to carry on his work.

She was born in Karachi on 21 June 1953, to Zulfikar's second wife, Nusrat. The Muslim family were 'feudals' – one of the important landowning families of Pakistan, sometimes called 'the twenty-two'. Educated by Catholic nuns at a convent school in her early years – as were, interestingly enough, several of the other leaders in this book, regardless of family religious background – Benazir Bhutto was sent abroad for her more advanced education.

She graduated from Harvard (cum laude) in 1973 with a degree in government; her father insisted that she continue on to Oxford, which he had attended. There she became the first foreign woman to be elected president of the Oxford Union, the university's famous debating society. Her father had also headed it in his day. She has called her years in England her happiest; by 1977, it was time to return home, to begin a career in diplomacy.

Instead, Bhutto found herself placed under house arrest or jailed, time after time for years, as she protested against her father's incarceration and the rule of the military. Hers were not country club jailings. At times she was in solitary confinement, suffering from extremes of heat and cold; poison was deliberately left in her cell as a temptation to suicide. At one point she was told that she might have uterine cancer, and subjected to an operation whose results were never made known to her. Pressure from abroad, and a dangerous ear infection, finally led to her being allowed to leave Pakistan for

London in January of 1984. From there she continued to protest against conditions at home, where 40,000 political prisoners were jailed.

Bhutto's opportunity to return to Pakistan came in April 1986. General Mohammed Zia ul-Haq, the martial law ruler, felt secure enough to allow political parties to operate once again. Huge crowds greeted Bhutto's return, and she campaigned for two years to build up her Pakistan People's Party, calling herself the 'sister' of her people. In 1987 she agreed to an arranged marriage with Asif Zardari, a businessman of similar social background. She felt that marriage was a necessity for political reasons; the marriage turned out to be a fulfilling one. The couple have three young children.

In the summer of 1988 General Zia was mysteriously killed in a plane crash. Bhutto and her mother (a member of parliament) led their party to victory in autumn elections. In December 1988 Bhutto once more followed in her father's footsteps. She became prime minister of Pakistan, the first woman ever to lead a modern Muslim state. Despite all that she had gone through, her real test was only just beginning.

To get to govern, Bhutto agreed not to reduce Pakistan's military budget nor to interfere in Afghan policy, which supported the Afghanistan guerrilla movement. The agreements reduced monies available for social programmes she had promised, but, in any case, her party had no majority in either house of parliament, and no legislation of significance was passed. She was able to remove restrictions on the press, trade unions, and student organizations, and to free from jail women who had been imprisoned under Pakistan's Hudood ordinances. But the ordinances – permitting women to be lashed or stoned for adultery (or for a rape *portrayed* as adultery) – remained in place. On 6 August 1990 Pakistan's president dismissed Bhutto as prime minister, one of his constitutional prerogatives.

She remained in the National Assembly as the leader of the opposition. In October of 1993, after three years of government crises and disputed elections, she was named prime minister for the second time. Major distractions were to include disputes with her mother and a brother returned from exile, over the latter's political role in a country where males are used to predominating over women. Bhutto has said that her chances for success in solving Pakistan's huge problems of illiteracy, poverty and female inequality are better this time around. Whatever her opportunities or policies, journalist Shazia Rafi wrote in *Ms* Magazine in November 1990 that Bhutto will be 'circumscribed by legacies from the past'.

GRO HARLEM BRUNDTLAND

Prime Minister, Norway

Norway's prime minister, a native of Oslo, impresses one immediately as someone who is in control and has a precise, analytical mind. Her name has come up as possible top secretary-general of the United Nations.

A pragmatist as well as an idealist, Brundtland can cap wages or devalue currency when necessary, but she is a strong defender of Norway's highly developed 'safety net'. As she is quoted as saying in *Time* magazine in September 1989, 'If you are born strong, with parents who give you the best, you have an even stronger responsibility for the people who didn't get the same start.'

The prime minister skis and sails. The story is often told of how, when her husband accidentally fell from their sailboat during a sail, and could not climb back on board, Dr Brundtland was able to bring him and their boat home through rough water after two hours of struggle.

It's very difficult to evaluate a leader in a very short-term perspective because to be a leader you must be able to have a long-term perspective. You must be able to carry changes which take many years. And this is why you can really only see whether it has been a good leadership after some years have passed.

GRO HARLEM BRUNDTLAND

Gro Harlem Brundtland, a medical doctor, has been Norway's prime minister on three separate occasions during the 1980s and 1990s – each time for a longer period than the last. She is a dominant presence in her country and has an international reputation for her environmental work with the United Nations.

Brundtland was born in a suburb of Oslo on 20 April 1939, one of four children. Her father was a physician who would hold cabinet posts in Labour governments, and both parents were political activists. Brundtland herself was involved in Labour activities by the age of seven, when she joined an affiliated youth group.

While attending medical school at Oslo University in 1960, Gro Harlem married Arne Brundtland, a political science student, and began her family of four children. The mid–1960s found both parents studying at Harvard, where Gro Brundtland took a master's degree in public health in 1965; environmental studies were part of her work.

Back in Norway, Brundtland held several government posts administering health care services. As she pointed out in her interview, it was her strong feelings about abortion rights for women which brought her to the public's attention when the issue was debated in Norway in the 1970s.

Appointment as Norway's minister of the environment in 1974 further increased her public recognition. The next year she was elected deputy leader of the Labour party. In 1979 she resigned her environmental post to enter the Storting (Parliament) and to work at building up her party. In February of 1981, after a Labour prime minister resigned, she was chosen by her party's central committee to be party head and hence her country's new prime minister, at the age of 41.

Her first term was short-lived – Labour lost elections in October and the Conservative party formed the next government. Brundtland remained in the Storting, and in 1984 began working with the United Nations World Commission on Environment and Development; she became chair. The commission held hearings on environmental problems in several countries around the world and issued the influential report *Our Common Future* in 1987.

Of all world leaders, probably very few can match Brundtland's grasp of the serious long-term implications of current environmental trends. She is equally concerned with justice for the Third World, and advocates much greater financial assistance to poorer nations, in part so that they can bypass the 'dirty' phases of development by using newer, cleaner technologies. As she said in an interview with the *UNESCO Courier* in 1990, 'the developing world will need increasing amounts of energy to provide for its economic and social development. This means that energy will have to be saved in the industrially developed countries ... We must aim for a type of economic growth which uses less energy and [fewer] natural resources. And this can only be done by agreement. There must be sufficient information and pressure from public opinion so that nations will get together and take decisions on this issue.'

Brundtland came back into the prime ministership (1986–89) when the Conservatives lost voting strength in 1986. Commentators like to note that she then formed the world's first 'gender-balanced cabinet', with eight women cabinet ministers and nine men. In her third period as head of government from 1990 to the present day, she matched this with nine women of nineteen ministers.

Dr Brundtland has said that political feminism starts in political parties, because 'in a political party the ideals of equality and how things should be are part of the process itself. You discuss what a society should be.'[1]

VIOLETA CHAMORRO

President, Nicaragua

In a hot Managua, a gracious Violeta Chamorro meets with me in a room whose furnishings include photographs of world leaders, well-crafted cowhide chairs, large potted plants and a life-size picture of her martyred husband. A security inspection had included the removal of a small pocketknife from my purse.

We are served water glasses wrapped in white linen; in return for my gift of a book of national park photographs, the President makes me a present of a carved gourd. She wears a green and black two-piece dress and prominent dangling earrings; her eyes are brown and her grey hair is stylishly cut.

> We're working together, have extended our hands to Nicaraguans, are working for reconciliation, are working for peace, are working to bring back all the Nicaraguans who ... left this country in the exodus.
>
> VIOLETA CHAMORRO

Violeta Barrios de Chamorro, elected to a six-year term as president of Nicaragua in 1990, inherited a divided nation. Her predecessor, Daniel Ortega, won the first internationally monitored, corruption-free elections that Nicaragua had held in decades, in 1984. But as Ortega's government continued to be opposed by the United States – which funded a fighting force (the Contras) against it for nearly a decade – war-weary voters looked to Chamorro to bring peace, an end to the draft and US aid for their ruined economy.

Chamorro is one of seven children, and was born into a wealthy landowning family on 18 October 1929, in Rivas. She still owns a 'very small piece' of the cattle ranch where she led a happy childhood, swimming in Lake Nicaragua and horseback riding with her father. Eventually her family sent her to the United States to attend Our Lady of the Lake Catholic School for Girls in San Antonio, Texas. She continued on to Blackstone College, in Virginia, but left within a year when her father died in 1948.

Back in Nicaragua, she was soon introduced to Pedro Joaquín Chamorro. The Chamorros, like the Barrios family, came from the country's wealthy landowning class; they had been active in Nicaraguan politics for generations. Pedro Chamorro began opposing a series of Somoza dictators while still a law student: his activities in the 1940s led to his being exiled, as were his parents, publishers of the newspaper *La Prensa*. The family was able to return to Nicaragua and re-open their paper by 1948.

Pedro and Violeta were married in 1950; they started a family of four children (a fifth child died). Pedro Chamorro, an extremely courageous man, used his pen and his organizing abilities against the Somozas for thirty years. His wife raised their children and took meals to prison on the occasions when her husband was jailed for his activities. When Pedro Chamorro was gunned down by assassins in 1978, his wife became *La Prensa*'s publisher.

Pedro Chamorro's death so outraged Nicaragua's business and professional classes that an historical turning point was reached. Peasant guerrillas and student and urban revolutionaries who had physically battled with the Somozas for years now had new allies. In the summer of 1979 the last of the Somozas fled abroad, to be assassinated in Paraguay. Nicaragua had had a successful revolutionary insurrection.

Unity was to be short-lived. The Sandinista Liberation Front, the dominant political force in the new revolutionary government, had different ideas for Nicaragua than did others who had joined in the anti-Somoza effort. The Sandinistas seized extensive Somoza properties, instituted land reform and began major health and literacy campaigns. Remnants of Somoza's police and military forces fled to the border with Honduras and were soon receiving money and arms from the US. By the early 1980s Nicaragua once again had fighting in its rural areas. Casualties mounted into many thousands.

Reflecting the divided state of their country, Violeta Chamorro's four adult children split evenly over Nicaragua's future. Two (Claudia and Carlos) actively supported Sandinista policies; two others (Pedro and Cristiana) actively opposed them. Cristiana's husband

– Antonio Lacayo – became Chamorro's chief campaign strategist and presidential adviser. Chamorro was often outspokenly anti-Sandinista, but kept her family together, speaking of her respect and love for all of her children, and of her desire to unify her people and move ahead. This capacity for caring beyond politics – illustrated by Chamorro's table at family dinners – is still an important civic model in Nicaragua.

When she took office, Chamorro ended the draft and greatly reduced the size of the Sandinista army. But some of her policies – notably, retaining Humberto Ortega, Daniel's brother, as army chief – alienated former political allies who had supported her presidential run. She travelled to the United States in May of 1991 to ask for at least ten years of financial aid. But substantial help for Nicaragua has not been forthcoming. Chamorro ended her interview by commenting: 'Some abroad do not understand what we are trying to do here; some do understand.'

MARY EUGENIA CHARLES
Prime Minister, Commonwealth of Dominica

Eugenia Charles is a lawyer who doesn't stand on ceremony. The first woman prime minister in the Caribbean once greeted a delegation of foreign conservationists wearing a house dress and low shoes, her head wrapped in a towel. She had just finished washing her hair in a waterfall behind her house.

The island which Charles governs, between Guadeloupe and Martinique, is known for its black volcanic beaches and rugged rainforest terrain. The extremely rare sisserou parrot – red, dark green, and violet – lives only here. Dominica is reached by a six-seater airplane from more developed islands of the Caribbean; landing on its small airstrip made some of my fellow-passengers nervous.

I was taken to Charles' small office in Roseau, the capital, by Harvey Royer, a cameraman whom she knows and who, in turn, seemed to know everyone on Dominica. Chickens and goats poked around by the car park. The prime minister speaks in a lilting West Indian voice; her manner is approachable, down-to-earth, forthcoming. She loves hanging plants, and requested some macramé hangers when asked what small gift I could bring her as a thank you for our interview.

To me equality is the important thing. I don't want preferences, I don't want to be preferred as a woman. But I want it acknowledged that I am a human being who has the capacity to do what I have to do, and it doesn't matter whether I was born a man or woman. The work will be done that way.

EUGENIA CHARLES

Eugenia Charles is usually described as one of five children of a 'well-to-do' family of Dominica – three brothers are doctors, her sister is a nun. In her interview for this book, Charles stressed her father's self-made roots:

People always describe me now as a daughter of a millionaire, my father was so rich. He wasn't. He worked very hard for what he had … he had only primary school education. So did my mother. But my father and mother really continued to educate themselves by their reading … as a child, I took it for granted. But looking back I realize how they were *always* reading.

Her father's belief that 'education was the answer to everything' is reflected in Charles' own education. Born on 15 May 1919, she first attended Catholic schools on Dominica and Grenada. When college time arrived, she set off for University College of the University of Toronto (1942–1946), receiving a bachelor's degree in law. From there she went to England to study at the Inner Temple, Inns of Court. She was called to the English Bar in 1947, and enrolled for additional study at the London School of Economics. She then became the only woman lawyer practising on Dominica.

An effort by the governing Dominica Labour Party to limit dissent with a sedition act in 1968 brought Charles actively into politics, and eventually led to the formation of her political party, the Dominica Freedom Party (DFP). In 1975 Charles, as its leader, became government opposition leader.

Dominica achieved its independence from Britain three years later, in 1978. Charles had warned that the country might not be ready for its new status. After a series of crises, the DFP won a very large electoral victory in the summer of 1980, and Charles became prime minister. The highly competent Charles has held the position ever since; her third term runs through 1995. According to journalist Myfanwy van de Veld, the DFP 'traditionally appealed to business and plantocracy interests, but since becoming prime minister Miss Charles has broadened that appeal very considerably and is now seen very much as a "leader of the people".' Dominica faces problems of poverty and underdevelopment.

Strongly anti-Communist, Charles encouraged the US invasion of Grenada. She was able to obtain millions of dollars from the US in the 1980s to build up Dominica's weak infrastructure. But Charles is not interested in the wrong kinds of development for her small, unspoiled island. She once told writer Anthony Weller: 'I won't have any package tours coming here and barging around. I've seen what mass tourism has done to other islands. It doesn't help the people financially or otherwise, and it ruins the place.' Dominica's motto (in Creole) is '*Après Bondie, c'est la Ter*' – 'After God, the Earth'.

TANSU CILLER
Prime Minister, Turkey

Tansu Ciller – interviewed in Ankara in June of 1994 – paid tribute to her husband's ability to be the mate of a woman in politics. She said that Ozer Ciller – a businessman and engineer with a master's degree in computer science – 'has his own preferences ... his own personality, but, despite everything, he stood up ... beautifully. And now, in a country like Turkey, people are talking more about this kind of thing than ever.'

Ciller is a lively woman who smiles frequently. She said that she was 'learning to have fun' at her job, despite 'all the adversities' – which have included sexist chants by her opponents: 'Tansu mutfaga' – 'Tansu back to the kitchen.'

I have been in ... parliament for [over two] years now, and I've been a prime minister for one year. We need more women in the parliament before I can have more women in the cabinet. We have [a] very low percentage of women in the parliament right now, and [in] 1996 we're going to have ... general elections. I'm hoping more women will participate ... The reason for that is not that I am a woman only ... when you take the women and the younger population, they're almost 75 to 80 percent of the population in my country, and therefore we need more women and young people ... to have a fairer ... representation of the population.

TANSU CILLER

Tansu Ciller became prime minister of Turkey, the world's only secular Muslim state, in June of 1993. She thus became the third woman to govern a modern Islamic nation, with Benazir Bhutto (Pakistan) and Khaleda Zia (Bangladesh) as her predecessors.

Turkey differs from other Muslim (and even some Western) countries in having a long historical tradition of women in the professions, dating back to the earlier twentieth century. Such women – often practising law or medicine – were born into Turkey's wealthier class, and lead lives very different from those of the mass of Turkish women. Ciller, aged 47 at the time of her appointment, is part of a continuing unique tradition.

Born in Istanbul, she is the daughter of a well-to-do provincial governor. She married early, after high school, and has two sons. Her husband, Ozer, took her family surname of Ciller. Tansu Ciller attended American-run Roberts College in Istanbul, then pursued further education in the United States. She earned a Ph.D. in economics at the University of Connecticut and did additional postgraduate work at Yale.

After her return from the US in 1974, Ciller began teaching economics at Istanbul's Bosporus University. She moved from academia to politics in 1991, when she became Turkey's economics minister, appointed by Süleyman Demirel, her predecessor as prime minister. She had earlier served as one of his advisers.

In the summer of 1993 Demirel's party, True Path, saw Ciller as someone who could bring a fresh image of youth, vigour, and change to the office of party head (and, subsequently, of prime minister). Demirel was quoted as saying that Ciller's selection by True Path 'shows that Turkey is a part of the Western world, that Turkey is a civilized country'.[2] According to *Lear's* magazine, Istanbul's teens break-danced at Ciller's victory celebration, chanting, 'Down with the fossils'.[3]

When she came to power, Ciller announced an attack on bureaucracy and on bribery. She also planned to privatize some Turkish state-run enterprises. In her interview, Ciller commented that money from privatization could build 'a lot of schools, a lot of hospitals'.

However, Ciller faced severe economic problems, as well as the issue of Kurdish separatism. She proposed to the Turkish parliament that Kurdish-language schools and radio broadcasts be legalized. The press reported visits from Turkish military officers warning her not to be soft on Turkish terrorists. In the spring and summer of 1994 such terrorists were setting off bombs in Istanbul, and human rights groups were denouncing Turkey's human rights record. Muslim fundamentalists – and their Welfare Party – were being viewed by some as a long-range threat to Turkey's secular politics and legal system. The state of Turkey's economy had worsened rather than improved.

According to Turkish researcher Sirin Tekeli, the strengthening of Turkey's economy is needed in order to produce more jobs for women of all classes – to overcome the economic dependence on family which has been the greatest traditional burden for women in Turkey.

EDITH CRESSON

Former Prime Minister, France

'One of the most obvious characteristics of the bourgeoisie is the boredom it produces.' This line from Edith Cresson's autobiography would have been well understood by French writer Simone de Beauvoir, a fellow rebel against middle class ennui and female restriction.

Edith Cresson's life has certainly not been dull. The elegant woman I interviewed – who was wearing a blonde suit and sitting in front of white shelves of *objets d'art* – has been pelted with tomatoes by French farmers who were resentful of her reforms of their protected markets. According to biographer Olga Opfell, while she was involved in promoting French trade, Cresson 'rode a French motor scooter to work to prove that French models were as good as ... popular Japanese ones.' The former prime minister likes to swim and bicycle.

> Even if [a man] does not succeed in accomplishing anything, it does not matter, because he asserts a certain number of things, or he presents himself as a leader in a way which ... corresponds to tradition. People expect of a woman results, and quick ones, if possible.
>
> EDITH CRESSON

Edith Cresson had already handled difficult assignments for President François Mitterrand when he appointed her France's first woman prime minister in May of 1991, making her potentially one of the most powerful women in Europe.

From 1981 to 1984 she served as France's Minister of Agriculture, absorbing tough comments from French farmers unaccustomed to a woman in that post. Later she took on a new portfolio, that of Industrial Restructuring and External Trade, at a time when the iron and steel industry was undergoing change: 'It was very hard ... I used to go to Lorraine every month to speak to the factory workers and the unions to try to make the transition easier.'[4]

Cresson was born on 27 January 1934, in a fashionable suburb of

Paris. Her parents, Gabriel and Jacqueline Campion, were well-off bourgeoisie who were to have two sons as well. Cresson's father worked for the French government. The family hired an English nanny for their daughter, and as a result she is bilingual in French and English.

Cresson's early life was shaped by conditions in France during World War II. Her father was working for the French embassy in Belgrade, Yugoslavia, when France fell to the Nazis. When the embassy was closed, he settled his family in Thonon-les-Bains, on Lake Geneva, and then returned to Paris. Edith Cresson was enrolled in a convent boarding school, Sacre Coeur.

She witnessed the fates of the French Jews and other persons under the Nazi-controlled French government: 'In the mountains, where I was sent on holiday and to be better nourished, the head of the house where I lived was deported and died in Mauthausen.'5 The distinction that Cresson likes to make between those who look respectable and those who are truly admirable came to her early as she saw 'the conforming middle class, and, on the other hand, people whom I knew to be in the Resistance.'5

When she was seventeen, Cresson was admitted to one of France's prestigious schools -the Haute École Commerciale (HEC) – where she took a business degree. In December of 1959 she married Jacques Cresson, an executive with Peugeot. The couple has two daughters. Edith Cresson later returned to HEC to earn her doctorate in demography. Her thesis was based on interviews with Breton farm women.

Cresson's career in politics began when she became a campaign worker in one of Mitterrand's early presidential campaigns in 1965. He lost, but ran again in 1974. Cresson joined his Socialist Party, and was asked to run for the National Assembly from Châtellerault, a conservative town in Vienne. She was expected to lose, and did, but was appointed to a party post. Soon after, she began to win elections and appointments.

In 1977 she was elected mayor of the city of Thure; in 1979 to the European Parliament; in 1981 to the National Assembly. In 1983 she even became mayor of Châtellerault, where she had lost her first race.

Meanwhile, Mitterrand finally won the French presidency in 1981, and asked his prime minister to award Cresson the agriculture portfolio. She continued on to other portfolios, including that of Minister of European Affairs.

After she was appointed prime minister, however, it was unclear whether France was ready for her, or she ready for France. Always very frank, Cresson did not change her style when she became head of government. Some topics of little significance on which she had once given her opinions to the press drew attention and denigration. She was satirized on a French television show as a cat, 'Amabotte', nuzzling the boots of Mitterrand. Her experience, seriousness and intelligence were overlooked as her popularity dropped in the polls. The Socialists began to see her as a liability, and in April of 1992 she resigned as prime minister. While initially silent about her treatment by the media and her party, Cresson later shared with a woman journalist her strong feelings of anger about her usage. A beautiful woman who embodies French chic, Cresson is now president of a Paris consulting firm, SISIE.

VIGDIS FINNBOGADÓTTIR
President, Iceland

The residence of Iceland's president is on a low promontory, outside Reykjavik, facing the sea. Verdant grounds and no obvious indications of security arrangements greeted us – rather, a friendly, warm housekeeper, who invited us in to sign a guest book, 'look around', and listen to her recitation of some Icelandic poetry. Iceland's people are proud of their literary heritage, as is their head of state.

'President Vigdis' is an articulate, attractive woman with short, blondish hair and dark blue eyes. Dressed in a white wool suit, she answered my questions in her fine library, and showed me some photo albums of her meetings with other world leaders. Iceland's small population means that the president knew even the cabdriver who delivered us to her residence – but, as she colourfully said, the importance of a country 'is not counted by hats'. Iceland, she believes, has messages for the world.

I think that the growing number of women as heads of state is due to the work women have done themselves to promote women, to prove to the world that women are in no way inferior to men when it comes to having important posts. It has been a great struggle to prove that, and to know that half of the world doesn't know that yet.

VIGDIS FINNBOGADÓTTIR

Vigdis Finnbogadóttir, elected President of Iceland in 1980, commented: 'They chose me because I'm a woman and in spite of my being a woman.' The former theatre director and television teacher has been re-elected every four years ever since.

Finnbogadóttir is Iceland's fourth (and only woman) head of state since Iceland became independent from Denmark in 1944. The president does not introduce legislation, and Finnbogadóttir does not even belong to a political party. Iceland's presidents serve as cultural ambassadors and symbols of national unity, although the Icelandic constitution also requires that they sign into law all bills passed by the parliament (Althing). No president has refused a signature to date, although Finnbogadóttir came close. In 1985 the Icelandic Women's Liberation Movement called a nationwide strike of women in Iceland, asking them to boycott their jobs or housework to protest against unequal wages for women, as well as other forms of discrimination. (According to a *New York Times* story on 25 October 1985, 'groups of men crowded into hotels in the early morning, after their wives refused to cook breakfast for them. Most of Iceland's telephone switchboards were left unstaffed.') Women flight attendants for Icelandic Air wanted to join in the boycott, but the Althing passed a bill forbidding it. Finnbogadóttir resisted signing this bill, but ultimately was argued into doing so. The flight attendants joined the boycott anyway.

Iceland's president was born in Reykjavik, the capital, on 15 April 1930. Her parents were professionals. Her father was an engineer and a professor at the University of Iceland; her mother, a nurse, was for many years chair of the Icelandic Nurses' Association. Finnbogadóttir began her college studies at home, but soon went abroad to study French language and literature at the University of Grenoble and at the Sorbonne. She also studied in Denmark (theatre history) and Sweden before returning to Iceland for work in English literature and in education.

She began a career teaching French at two of Iceland's junior colleges, then became an instructor in French drama at the University of Iceland. At this time she also became a teacher on the state television network, giving French lessons and speaking on drama. In 1972 her deep interest in theatre led to her appointment as director of the Reykjavik Theatre Company. She knows Iceland's playwrights well, and wishes that their work were more frequently translated.

In 1980 Finnbogadóttir was heavily lobbied to run for president by people who felt that the time for a woman head of state had arrived. Divorced and a single mother (she adopted a daughter, Astridur, when she was 41) she found these features of her personal life no handicap in her campaign: 'I think people liked it that I had the eccentricity to adopt a child as a single woman.'[6]

Women in Iceland keep their maiden names when they marry. The president's last name derives from her father's first name, Finnbogi, and has no connection to her early marriage. She is known in Iceland as President Vigdis.

Highly cultured and very conversant with Icelandic history, in interviews Finnbogadóttir declines to discuss the sensitive political subjects which are not considered to be part of her presidential arena. But like President Mary Robinson of Ireland – another 'nonpolitical' head of state – she is well aware of the significance of her position. As she told *Scandinavian Review* the week after her first inauguration:

> I'm convinced that the fact of a woman winning the presidential election here will help women in my country, as well as women in other countries. I can already see that from the many letters I've received from women all over the world. They've taken note of my election and

they think that it's exciting and encouraging … It's time women stood together. We can't wait another 20 years. It's wrong to wait too long and think that things will change tomorrow. We have to change them today.

MARIA LIBERIA-PETERS
Former Prime Minister, Netherlands Antilles

The office of the prime minister of the Netherlands Antilles was located in a Dutch Colonial-style building on the waterfront in Willenstad – a colourful city painted in Caribbean pastels. Children's drawings on a wall recall Liberia-Peters' former profession. Framed photos speak of her interest in photography.

The former prime minister's ethos is that of the dedicated public servant; she is clear, intelligent and likeable, noted for keeping people informed and playing fair. It seemed not inappropriate that, while I was in her home town, the Caribbean Association for Feminist Research and Action sponsored a poetry reading to celebrate the publication of *Creation Fire*, an anthology of Caribbean women's poetry.

I've realized that you cannot reach your goal without power. So it's not a nasty word, it's an important word. But you must know what you want to do with that power. Serve mankind, serve for humanity, and then, yes, give me all the power in the world.

MARIA LIBERIA-PETERS

Maria Liberia-Peters, the first woman prime minister of the Netherlands Antilles, is a popular leader known for her abilities to convince and build consensus. The former kindergarten teacher was born Maria Peters on 20 May 1941, in Willenstad, Curaçao, Netherlands Antilles. Her husband, Niels, is a civil servant. The couple adopted two young children, now teenagers, through the Roman Catholic Archdiocese of New York.

The former prime minister speaks four languages (Dutch, English, Spanish, and Papiamento – the latter a mixture of the first three plus Portuguese, seasoned with Arawak and African additions). Liberia-Peters was educated in Europe.

> I did my teacher's degree in Holland. I worked for five years [starting in 1962] in early childhood education, and then went back for training in pedagogy and became a teacher in training college here. And then I said farewell to teaching ... I expect some day I will be back in the classroom.

As she explained further, Liberia-Peters' position as a teacher made her aware of the social needs of students and their families. She organized parents' groups for political and social action, and joined a political party (the NVP – National People's Party). After she was approached to run for office, she won a seat on the Curaçao island council in 1975. That body named her (1975–80) to an executive council which met regularly with Queen Beatrix's representative. The Netherlands Antilles is an autonomous, self-governing region which is part of the Kingdom of the Netherlands, with Holland responsible for defence and foreign affairs.

In 1982 Liberia-Peters was elected to the Staten (legislature) of the Netherlands Antilles, and also became Minister of Economic Affairs in a coalition government which collapsed in June of 1984. In September she was asked to form a new coalition government; she took office as prime minister that month. Her first period as prime minister lasted until 1986, when political events intervened to make her, instead, leader of the opposition. She came back into the prime ministership in the spring of 1988.

The 1980s brought difficult economic times to the Netherlands Antilles, a country of five islands (Curaçao, Bonaire, Sint Maarten, Saba and Sint Eustatius) north of Venezuela. The economy had traditionally been heavily dependent upon two oil refineries which refined Venezuelan oil. One refinery, Exxon's, closed in 1984; Netherlands Antilles was able to keep a Shell refinery operating by taking it over on advantageous terms and leasing it to a Venezuelan oil company, PDVSA.

During these and other economic hardships, which included high unemployment, Liberia-Peters told the *New York Times* in August 1985:

> What I really hope is that I will be successful in at least setting out the lines for the future, for a new future, so that the people of the Netherlands Antilles can say 'OK, we're going through a difficult situation, but nevertheless this is where it's going to lead ... there is light.' It's a situation you have to handle very carefully, so that my people don't panic. As the Spanish people say, I have to keep away *la desesperación* – the desperation.

The islands now seek a diversified economy partially grounded in different forms of tourism; Bonaire is, for instance, known as a scuba divers' paradise.

The burdens of office have not prevented Liberia-Peters from having fun. Her self-confidence as a leader was demonstrated when she declined to watch the annual Carnival parade from the prime minister's traditional place in a reviewing stand, and instead danced in the parade (as she had done for the previous seven years), wearing pink and green lamé. She told the *New York Times* that she had 'struggled' with the decision, but 'knew she would not feel happy as a spectator ... standing at the side.' Although some people felt her dancing was not appropriate, said the prime minister: 'In the first place I'm Maria, and in the second place I'm prime minister. So I'm going.' In the spring of 1994 the National People's Party lost elections, so Liberia-Peters moved into a role she has played before, leader of the opposition.

KAZIMIERA PRUNSKIENE

Former Prime Minister, Lithuania

Vilnius, in January of 1994, reminded me of Russia. There were wide boulevards, and the hard-to-spot shops containing limited, imported consumer goods. Some of the vegetables for sale had come from too near Chernobyl, I was told, so that many people refused to buy them. Residents shrug in response to their difficult conditions.

Kazimiera Prunskiene, Lithuania's former prime minister, invited me to dine with her at a local restaurant, subsequent to our interview, and even played chauffeur, driving a small old car. A charming woman with reddish hair and a wide collection of stories, Prunskiene has written a book about her experiences, *Cost of Freedom*.

I think that a very important feature [of a leader] would be ... experience in state matters. It's very difficult to imagine a person coming to politics, to the state level, by chance – the person who has no earlier, no previous experience as a leader, even on a lesser level.

KAZIMIERA PRUNSKIENE

Kazimiera Prunskiene was prime minister of Lithuania during nine critical months in which her Baltic country sought to establish its independence from the Soviet Union.

She was born on 26 February 1943, in the village of Vasiuliskiai. World War II-Lithuania was at that time occupied by the Germans. As she stated in her interview, Prunskiene lost her father at the age of one; her mother raised three children alone. Despite whatever challenges these circumstances presented to the family, Prunskiene was educated to a high level. She gained a degree from the University of Vilnius in 1965 in economics; she stayed on to teach. In the 1980s she received a doctorate in her field; she has three children. She was eventually divorced from their father, and remarried later in 1989. She joined the Lithuanian Communist Party in 1980.

Lithuania's was a difficult history. In the 1920s, its first president,

A Smetona, became dictatorial. In 1940 the USSR annexed the country; then the Germans invaded. In 1944 the USSR re-invaded and annexed Lithuania once again.

In the 1980s came the new and influential ideas of *perestroika* (restructuring) put forth by Soviet President Mikhail Gorbachev. Prunskiene became a founding member of Sajudis (the Lithuanian Restructuring Movement); it was to become the main pro-independence group in Lithuania. However, independence came only in stages and after much struggle.

By 1989 Prunskiene was very busy: she was a minister in the still Soviet-controlled Lithuanian government, an elected member of the USSR Supreme Soviet, and an active member of Sajudis. In these forums she was, according to biographer Olga Opfell, 'energetic', 'forceful' and 'a skilled debater'.

President Gorbachev, despite his restructuring policies, wanted to keep Lithuania within the orbit of the USSR. But huge street demonstrations occurred in Vilnius, and in March of 1990 the Lithuanian parliament (Supreme Council) voted for independence. Six days later it appointed Prunskiene to be prime minister.

Prunskiene seems at first to have underestimated the possible reaction of her 'dear friend' Gorbachev to Lithuania's declaration of independence. After an embargo of oil, gas, and raw materials was declared by Moscow against her country in mid-April, she set off on travels to the US and several European capitals, asking for their intervention on Lithuania's behalf in her negotiations with Moscow. She finally met with Gorbachev for talks on 17 May, but his offer of independence in two years was not accepted.

Moscow's boycott damaged the Lithuanian economy. Prunskiene was able to end it after two and a half months by getting the Supreme Council to agree to suspend independence while negotiations were active with the USSR. She also urged controversial free-market economic reforms within Lithuania. Conflict continued during all of 1990; one focus was the issue of Lithuanian 'draft evaders' from the Soviet army: the Supreme Council had decided they had no obligation to serve.

In January 1991 events moved towards a new state of crisis. Prunskiene met again in Moscow with President Gorbachev, but did not receive assurances that the Soviet army would not be used against Lithuania. On the same day, she learned that some of her economic policies had been rejected by her parliament at home. Prunskiene resigned as prime minister. Nine months later Boris Yeltsin came to power in Moscow, and the USSR recognized the independence of the three Baltic republics.

Prunskiene stayed active as a member of parliament in 1991 and 1992, after which she withdrew from the public arena, drawing upon her background in economics to work as a consultant.

Economic problems continue to afflict Lithuania. The Baltic states are among Europe's poorest, and, as in Russia, the movement away from Soviet-style economic arrangements towards a free-market economy has lowered living standards for many and brought problems of crime and Mafia-style extortion and violence. As a result, Sajudis lost the elections in November of 1992. The Democratic Labour Party – successor to the former Communist Party of Lithuania – came into power. Two years later this government was applying for membership in NATO.

MARY ROBINSON
President, Ireland

A light which the President of Ireland keeps burning at all hours on the second floor of the presidential mansion is her chosen signal to Irish people living abroad that they have a tie to their homeland and are remembered there. Even today, because of the dearth of jobs at home, Ireland's citizens compete in a lottery to migrate to the United States.

'Caring' is one of the first words that comes to mind to describe President Robinson; one is struck by her deep sincerity as a humanitarian idealist. She concluded her official interview by commending the work of Irish author Roddy Doyle, saying that hers was 'a complete book family'. Then she invited us for refreshments, and a look at her 'favourite room', leading the way in a red and green plaid suit and black stockings.

You move politics along by being able to inject a sense of vision about certain values. Take, for example, relations on this island. If it's possible to project the values of pluralism, of respect for difference, of accommodating and finding space for difference, that should influence the policies of a political framework for peace and reconciliation.

MARY ROBINSON

When Mary Robinson started her campaign to become president of Ireland, the odds against her were considered to be 100 to 1. She was an intellectual activist whose views were often at odds with those of Ireland's conservative, Catholic-dominated culture. The 'leading candidates' were men, sponsored by Ireland's two largest parties. The presidency had become something of a sinecure for retiring male politicians, whereas Robinson was known as a woman reformer.

Mary Robinson won. She declared her 1990 victory 'a great, great day for Irish women', and said: 'The women of Ireland, instead of rocking the cradle, rocked the system.' How *did* she win? Three factors seem key: her particular qualities as a human being; her campaign's hard work – she extended the traditional campaign season by many weeks, and travelled all over Ireland in her campaign bus; a bit of luck: the voting system was complicated and rather unusual, giving Robinson the votes of the person third in line to add to her own second-place totals. Ireland now seems proud that it has elected Mary Robinson: reports on her activities glow with enthusiasm, and even her defeated main opponent has spoken approvingly of her job performance.

Robinson comes from a well-off Catholic family from County Mayo. She was born in Ballina, on 21 May 1944; both of her parents were physicians, although her mother stopped practising medicine to raise five children. Robinson's four brothers and she all attended Trinity College, Dublin, a predominantly Protestant institution. Robinson took a BA in French and then a law degree, compiling such an outstanding academic record that she was given a scholarship to Harvard to do graduate work in law. She has said that the year of study at Harvard – in 1968 – was particularly important to her development, largely because there was so much questioning of social institutions going on there, and in the United States generally, at that time.

When she returned to Ireland, Robinson, at 25, became the youngest law professor in the history of Trinity College. She also entered the upper house of the Irish parliament, running as a Labour candidate. She served there for twenty years, continually challenging Ireland's severe prohibitions against divorce, abortion, homosexuality and even the sale of contraceptives; in 1985 legislation was finally passed in Ireland allowing the purchase of contraceptives without a doctor's prescription. In 1991, the year after she was elected President, Robinson received word that some of her former legal work had resulted in the biggest equal-pay settlement for women in the country's history.

She holds personal views on feminism. Married to a former Trinity College classmate, Nicholas Robinson (a Protestant), and the mother of three children, she insists that true feminism allows each woman to go her own way: 'We've gone beyond the stage of simply wanting more women in particular positions ... It's much deeper than that and much more fundamental.' She once asked a journalist: 'If feminists don't value the work of the women who stay at home, how is society going to value it?'

Robinson finds being president particularly interesting *because* it is a restricted position: Ireland's president does not initiate legislation and cannot give a speech or leave the country without permission from the prime minister. But Robinson is finding many 'symbolic' ways to assert her values of tolerance, pluralism and human concern. She does this through the places she chooses to visit, both inside and outside of Ireland, and through the groups she invites to the presidential residence in Phoenix Park. She travelled to Northern Ireland to meet with an IRA leader in the interest of peace-seeking; she travelled to Somalia and published her private travel diary to raise funds for relief; at Christmas time in 1992 she welcomed 34 representatives of Ireland's gay and lesbian organizations to a special reception at her residence.

She has spoken frequently of the challenging language of 'symbols':

> What I've learned is the importance of symbols – as long as they are grounded in values. This office works on two levels. One is the level of values above politics, for example, offering the hand of friendship to the two communities in Northern Ireland. The other is below the political: meeting small groups concerned with community self-development. Unless I'm in touch at that level, I won't know the symbols. It's important to listen ... a phrase you use is appropriate only when you've been listening – in touch with the small print of people's lives.

HANNA SUCHOCKA
Former Prime Minister, Poland

While she was prime minister of Poland, Hanna Suchocka was said by the press to have presented an image of calm and control, even though aides knew the burdens of office could drive her to tears. The woman I met was hospitable and very honestly responsive, indicating disagreement where necessary and also sharing stories of her travels in the United States – where she disliked skyscrapers, but enjoyed Nevada.

She is single and a practising Catholic who refuses photo-opportunities inside churches; the former prime minister supports abortion only in extreme circumstances such as a threat to the mother's life.

I had to look for balance between seven political parties. For me it was not important [if] there were men or women ... the parties were so different that for me it was problem number one ... the problem of man and woman was [in] the second place, it was background.

HANNA SUCHOCKA

Hanna Suchocka was born into a Poland that had only recently come under the dominance of Moscow. Her life parallels that of the emergence of an independent Poland – with Suchocka, a popular prime minister, presiding over a recent phase of free-market reforms.

She comes from a highly cultured family with a background in politics – one of her grandmothers, for example, was a government minister as far back as 1919. Suchocka speaks several languages and plays the piano; she has said that music, poetry, history, and the Catholic religion were important in her home. Her parents ran a pharmacy; it had been founded by a grandfather who also lectured on pharmaceutical botany at the University of Poznán.

Suchocka was born on 3 April 1946, in Pleszew, in western Poland. Her parents hoped she would continue the family tradition in pharmacy, but Suchocka chose to study law, as did her younger sister, Elzbieta.

After Hanna Suchocka finished her law studies at the University of Poznán in 1968, she was given a teaching position there for one year, but her contract was not renewed after she refused to join the requisite political party. Instead, she joined another, smaller party, and pursued further study. In 1975 she obtained a doctoral degree in constitutional law from her alma mater and subsequently became a university lecturer.

In 1980 Suchocka became a member of the Communist parliament. It was the year that Solidarity – the trade union movement which was to embody the national drive for democratic freedoms – was born in Poland. The country came under martial law in December of 1981 as the government struck back at Solidarity and forced it underground. Lech Walesa and other leaders were interned. In 1984 Suchocka left parliament when her term expired; she had refused to vote for punitive measures against Solidarity.

The situation in Poland changed considerably after President Mikhail Gorbachev introduced reforms in the Soviet Union in the late 1980s. Political agreements in Poland led to elections in June of 1989, which were won by Solidarity-backed candidates: Suchocka was one of them. She joined the Democratic Union party, which was headed by Tadeusz Mazowiecki, the new prime minister. In 1990 Mazowiecki and Lech Walesa both ran for president of Poland, with Walesa the victor. In 1991 Suchocka was elected to a four-year term in the lower house of parliament (the Sejm).

Legislating in the Sejm was difficult because of the multitude of parties represented there – nearly 30 parties in 1992. (The voting system has since been changed to require that a party win at least five percent of an election in order to be represented.) Coalition governing was inevitable, with skill required to put the coalitions together. President Walesa went through three prime ministers before Suchocka's name was presented to him in July of 1992. She became his fourth prime minister.

Suchocka is a strong believer in the free-market reforms which have been underway in Poland over the past four years. The reforms have produced one of the highest levels of economic growth in all of Europe, but have also resulted in high unemployment and great hardship for pensioners, farmers, and public sector employees, including teachers and nurses. An unemployment rate of more than 15 percent in August of 1993 led to Suchocka's party being rebuffed at the polls in September of that year, despite her personal popularity. Voters turned back to the Communist Left, as happened in Lithuania – in effect, asking for a slowdown in reform policy.

Suchocka, still in parliament, has said that governing is 'a bit like mushrooms after the rain. Solve one problem and the next day, two, four, eight spring up.'

LADY MARGARET THATCHER

Former Prime Minister, United Kingdom of Britain and Northern Ireland

I met with Lady Margaret Thatcher at her office in an elegant area of London. A policeman was on guard at the front steps; a small statue of Sir Winston Churchill graced the office mantelpiece. Lady Thatcher wore a two-piece blue suit which set off her flashing blue eyes; her quick mind and debater's skill were evident throughout our conversation. Afterwards, she graciously invited me to tea.

The former prime minister shared memories of her childhood, during which the influence of her father in particular had played a dominant role: 'We were taught to read the papers and discuss the issues of the day ... We only rarely went to a film, and it had to be a good film ... Not necessarily a terribly learned one – for example, we did go to see Fred Astaire and Ginger Rogers because [the] dancing was just exquisite – but ... you were expected to make your own entertainment ... We weren't allowed [children's news-papers] full of the comic strips. Those were not permitted in the house.'

There's no point in getting too sensitive if you're in politics. What you've got to discern is that what you're doing can be justified by principle, by argument, and [to try] to put it across. That's the important thing.

LADY MARGARET THATCHER

Margaret Thatcher – the first woman to become head of a modern European government – also became Britain's longest-serving prime minister in the twentieth century. Other women leaders are invariably compared to her.

Both her family background and college politics shaped Thatcher's intense interest in government and governing. She was born in Grantham, in Lincolnshire, on 13 October 1925, the second daughter of a small-town grocer, Alfred Roberts, and his wife Beatrice. Her father, a Methodist lay preacher, was very active in his community, and served in a variety of civic positions, including those of alderman and mayor. According to Olga Opfell, at the time when her father was a part-time justice of the peace, 'Margaret often accompanied him to the courthouse, where she was so fascinated by the unfolding legal dramas that she thought she had erred in choosing a future in science.' But a family friend told her to get a chemistry degree before she studied law. She did.

Alfred Roberts believed in giving his daughters a good education, something that had been denied him. Margaret was the academic daughter, doing well in school and absorbing her adored father's advice and values – thrift, hard work, independence, success. At 17, she entered Somerville College, Oxford, where she joined and became president of the Oxford Union Conservative Association. After her graduation, she became a research chemist for a plastics firm, but also began to plan her political future.

Staying involved with the Conservative Party, she became a candidate for Parliament, but lost her first two races in 1950 and 1951. But her political activities led to her meeting Denis Thatcher, a businessman. The couple married in December 1951; Margaret gave birth to twins, a daughter and a son, two years later. By then she was studying law, and she was called to the bar the next year. Her specialities became tax and patent law.

In 1959 Thatcher made her third bid for a seat in Parliament, and won. Her maiden speech was impressive, and her hard work, energy and command of statistics were noticed by Conservative leaders, who had few women in their party. She was made shadow minister for several portfolios, following the British custom in which the party out of power creates a mirror cabinet of the party in office.

When the Conservatives *did* come to power, in 1970, Thatcher was made Secretary for Education, where she quickly became a controversial figure by cancelling the free milk allowance for schoolchildren, in line with Conservative intent to reduce government spending.

The Conservatives lost the general election in 1974, and Thatcher decided to enter the battle to choose a new party leader. She won in February 1975, having outpolled several other candidates. With a

Conservative victory in 1979, she became prime minister for the first time; she won her second term in 1983, and her third in 1987.

Many of Thatcher's basic goals in office were similar to those of President Ronald Reagan in the United States: reducing government spending and regulation; lowering taxes for businesses and the better-off; curbing the power of labour unions (whose membership dropped from 50 percent to 35 percent of the labour force during Thatcher's three terms). She also moved to privatize many of Britain's publicly owned industries. Friendships with Reagan and Soviet President Mikhail Gorbachev enabled her to play a role in ending the Cold War.

A different war consolidated her power during her first term as prime minister. Patriotic Britain rose behind Thatcher as she fought the brief 1982 Falkland Islands war against Argentina. Michael Genovese has written that 'the Falkland victory proved to be the seminal event in Thatcher's years in power. She was now seen as *the* leader of Britain ...'

But Thatcher's period of prime ministership ended when she was challenged from within for leadership of the Conservative Party. Economic problems, foreign policy issues (including her positions against European integration), and an unpopular poll tax which Thatcher championed (adopted, but since abandoned) resulted in a change of party leadership in November of 1990. Thatcher supported John Major, who became head of the Conservatives – but Thatcher has since become disenchanted with his leadership.

Thatcher briefly remained in Parliament after stepping down as prime minister, but soon became a member of the House of Lords, after her elevation to the peerage by the queen. The position gives her a platform from which to speak out on international issues, as she has done on Bosnia. She has published the first volume of her memoirs, and heads the Thatcher Foundation, dedicated to helping emerging private businesses in Eastern Europe.

KHALEDA ZIA
Prime Minister, Bangladesh

Prime Minister Zia has been described as being rather shy. But she believes that her self-effacing style is welcomed by her people, because it contrasts with the style of past military dictators. An air of dignity characterized her presence when I interviewed her in her nicely appointed office, complete with computer. She wore a white and black sari with a traditional head scarf.

I can tell you that whenever there is a woman leader at the helm of affairs, they face it with courage and determination ... women work with patience and they need cooperation.

KHALEDA ZIA

East Bengal became East Pakistan became Bangladesh. The retiring wife of a military officer became the widow of a president became a party leader and prime minister of her largely Islamic nation.

Khaleda Zia was raised as one of five children, the daughter of a businessman and his social worker wife, born to them on 14 August 1945. She grew up in East Bengal, attended primary and secondary schools, and, at the age of 15, married a captain in the Pakistani army, Zia-ur Rahman. The couple had two sons.

Pakistan's turbulent politics – which featured military takeovers, engineered elections and the successful revolt of East Pakistan from West Pakistan (to become Bangladesh in 1971) – were to frequently affect the life of Zia-ur Rahman. However, he also advanced in his military career, and by 1975 was military chief of staff. One coup and one assassination later, Zia was given several portfolios in a martial law administration. He was eventually elected president of Bangladesh, and founded the Bangladesh Nationalist Party (BNP).

On 30 May 1981, President Zia and two aides were shot while they slept in a military guest house, victims of a disgruntled general. In March of 1982, Bangladesh saw the coming to power of HM

Ershad in yet another military coup. Martial law was declared once more, and political parties were abolished. But the BNP continued to exist, with Khaleda Zia coming into politics as vice chair, then as party chair in 1984.

From 1984 until 1990, when Ershad finally resigned, Khaleda Zia was involved in constant protest efforts to end martial law and restore free elections. She was involved in street protests, strikes and mass demonstrations. She was placed under house arrest more than once. Ershad was ultimately forced out and arrested; fair elections in February of 1991 were won by the BNP, and Khaleda Zia became prime minister in March. Later that same year, a national referendum endorsed a new, parliamentary form of government for Bangladesh.

Since taking office, Khaleda Zia has given top priority to population control, mass literacy, compulsory primary education, the alleviation of poverty and rural electrification. Bangladesh is the ninth largest and fifth poorest of the world's nations; fewer than half of its 120 million people are literate, fewer than one third of its women. Yet population rates are dropping, and the country is being cited as a key example of how family planning programmes can be made to work even in the world's most impoverished nations.

According to journalist Barbara Crossette, writing in the *New York Times* on 17 October 1993: 'The country has begun to turn around, international development organizations say. At the World Bank, nobody calls Bangladesh a basket case any more.' In the same article, the prime minister is quoted as follows: 'It is a wrong conception that Islam is against family planning ... That may be true of the Catholics, but not Muslims. There is nothing in Islam that accepts that convention.'

CHAPTER 2

Politics Sans Intention

It never occurred to me in my entire life
that I would be here in this position.

VIOLETA CHAMORRO

As we have seen, roughly a quarter of the women interviewed for this book came to their top leadership positions through one of the most painful and unexpected of all routes: the assassination of their politically active husbands. Wives were asked to pick up the work of the fallen leader, sometimes after a number of years had passed, often more quickly.

It is no small assignment to be given.

In Nicaragua in the 1970s Violeta and Pedro Chamorro had been married for 27 years and had four grown children when Nicaragua's leading newspaperman was gunned down in his car – on 10 January 1978 – while driving to work at his newspaper. Pedro Joaquín Chamorro – a member of one of Nicaragua's most prominent families – had worked tirelessly and with great courage to rid his country of a series of Somoza-family dictators. His efforts had not been limited to journalism, but had meant organizing political opposition groups and even for a brief time taking up arms with a resistance force. He had been imprisoned, in exile, and threatened with death; he predicted he would be killed.

So potent an event was his martyrdom that his widow was invited into a governing coalition when the Sandinista Liberation Front completed the anti-Somoza revolution in July of 1979, 19 months after Pedro Chamorro's death. Violeta Chamorro's involvement with this coalition was short-lived, but even 11 years later, feuding groups wishing to oust the Sandinistas in the 1990 presidential elections turned to Mrs Chamorro – Nicaragua's 'mother' – as their best hope of a unifying figure.

In the Philippines in the 1980s Corazon Aquino played a similarly unifying role. When her husband Benigno returned home after three years of political exile in the United States – on 21 August 1983 – to attempt a renewed involvement in his country's politics of 'guns, goons, and gold', he was shot in the head before he could even leave Manila airport.

Corazon Aquino, still in exile, quickly returned to the Philippines to lead thousands of people in processions of mourning and protest. She then continued on to support several National Assembly candidates who were opposing the policies of dictator Ferdinand Marcos. Within two years, Aquino was seen as a figure who could unify leadership and mobilize the electorate to get rid of her dead husband's persecutor.

In her interview for this book, Aquino – for many years a shy, very private mother raising five children – described the reluctance she felt in taking on such a leading role as challenging Ferdinand Marcos for the presidency of her country. When we met, one of the prominent colours in her multi-flowered dress – yellow – reminded me: yellow ribbons had welcomed her husband home from exile, and yellow had been the colour she wore to campaign.

AQUINO: I was a reluctant candidate ... as you probably know, and I really was hoping, up to the very last, that it would be somebody else other than me. But the circumstances and the situation called for somebody who would be able to unite the opposition, and it was perceived that I alone would be able to do that ... here was a dictator who had really done much wrong to our people, and who, for 20 years, had ruled the country and had robbed the country from a better condition. And here were the people asking, you know, that they be liberated from this dictator and wanting that their rights and freedom be restored. My husband had been imprisoned for more than seven years, and then he had been assassinated. And I, at the beginning, I thought I would just support the opposition and not take the lead.

Q: That must have been quite a day when you went, in your own mind, from this notion of joining the group to leading the group.

AQUINO: Oh yes. In fact, I kept looking for reasons or excuses to get out of it ... but then once I had accepted the challenge, certainly I put heart and soul into it, and I certainly worked feverishly, first of all to win in the campaign, given such a formidable enemy as my predecessor. So it was, for me, not only a challenge, but perhaps a mission.

Aquino's sense of *mission* carried her to a dramatic victory – and many challenges as president for one six-year term, a constitutional limitation of the new post-Marcos constitution.

AQUINO: I always thought of myself as just being good for that one term. And, as I said, my mission was to restore democracy, and I was able to do that, with the help of the people, of course. So I felt that I had done my part and that it was time for me to move on to other activities. And also to accept the fact that perhaps somebody can do better than I.

When she left office, Aquino described to a Filipina journalist her relief at becoming a private citizen once again.

The heavy burden has been removed from me. I do not have to worry about my decisions, that they will affect many people. Whatever bad decision I make, only me or my family will be affected.[1]

The strain of being asked to lead was felt by another South Asian woman when Solomon Bandaranaike, prime minister of Ceylon (now Sri Lanka), was shot at his home by a Buddhist monk on 25 September 1959. The prime minister had been readying himself for a trip to the United States, where he was to speak at the United Nations and meet with President Eisenhower. He died the next day. The mother of three children, his widow Sirimavo told me of the hardship of playing the role she was then asked to take on.

I had no intention to take up politics during his life. Except after he died, people wanted me. I was more or less forced to take it up competitively . . . to lead the party after his death. I did not want to. But after much consideration, I agreed to take up the leadership of the party. Because of my discipline, I was able to do that, and take the party forward. And the discipline is all I had to lead the party politically – in 1960 – when I became the first woman prime minister of the world, as you know.

And, finally, Khaleda Zia, another woman who had led a secluded life and raised children, was also asked – within months after her husband's death – to involve herself in leading his political party. After rising through the military ranks to a political career and leadership role as an elected president, Zia-urRahman was shot down by an army general on 30 May 1981.

Violeta Chamorro, Corazon Aquino, Sirimavo Bandaranaike and Khaleda Zia could not foresee their political roles, nor plan for their political burdens. Aquino, Bandaranaike and Zia – along with Indira Gandhi and Benazir Bhutto, the prime minister of Pakistan – are often spoken of as inheritors of a kind of family dynastic politics typical of South and Southeast Asia.[2] Such women come from prominent families in which power is passed from one family member to the next, and gender is less important than family prominence. When Mrs Gandhi was herself assassinated, the mantle of power in India passed to her son Rajiv – who was sworn in as prime minister within hours of his mother's death.

It should be noted, though, that a tradition of husband-to-wife succession is not unique to Asia, nor to Latin America. While Brazil – like Nicaragua – has had a variant of the 'widow's succession,'[3] so too have the United States and Britain, among other countries. In England, 'common routes to political power are as the widow of a member [of Parliament] or as the wife of a member who moves to the House of Lords.'[4] In the US it has been pointed out that, 'in the first generation after suffrage, some two-thirds of the few women to serve in Congress were there because their husbands had died while in office and their governors had appointed them to finish their late husbands' terms.'[5] It seems safe to say that the mantle of power could not pass from a husband to a wife if the woman were not perceived as possessing certain necessary personal qualifications. These might or might not include leadership experience.

What *is* a leader, and what *are* the qualities needed to govern successfully? Leadership is often defined as the ability to move other people – followers – in a direction that is mutually desired.[6] To do so may require a multitude of skills – for example, a capacity to argue persuasively; powerful analytical insight; a full grasp of how one's political system operates; the ability to arouse feeling; the knowledge of when to call in one's debts.

Qualities of personality and character may be overriding: Does a person compromise too little or too much? Does a leader's behaviour carry moral authority or lack it? Does a leader inspire fear? Reverence? And since all leaders face huge constraints, how can a leader act so as to minimize resistance? One scholar, for example, has described how Indira Gandhi – despite her eminent family tree – 'continually encountered male hostility directed at her gender. The disrespect ranged from despair among some Indians over having a woman leader to sexist overtones in the contempt expressed by her critics, as in ... Pakistani President Yahya Khan's outburst during the Bangladesh conflict, "If that woman thinks she is going to cow me down, I refuse to take it."'[7] So, for a woman political leader, part of her preparation must simply mean thinking through what she could be up against.

As I discovered, most of the presidents and prime ministers interviewed for this book did not plan to be what they became. On the contrary, many found themselves – at some point along an evolutionary pathway – urged into leadership by others, because of obvious qualities which they possessed and displayed. Some leaders expressed surprise at where they had ended up.

Kazimiera Prunskiene became prime minister of Lithuania, and negotiated the future of her Baltic country with Mikhail Gorbachev.

Q: Was there anyone, when you were younger, who had been in politics that you admired?

49

PRUNSKIENE: When I was younger I did not admire politics at all. And I was not interested in the politics of that time. I was more interested in books and theatre, but not in politics. And even when I was choosing my profession I thought of choosing one far . . . from . . . politics.

Hanna Suchocka of Poland comes – like Prunskiene – from a country whose fate changed drastically in the late 1980s and 1990s. Suchocka, a highly educated law professor with parliamentary experience, showed some of the same reluctance about coming to the top as newly widowed Sirimavo Bandaranaike or Corazon Aquino.

SUCHOCKA: I ask myself . . . was it really necessary for me to be prime minister? I put the question, but it is a question for me.

Q: I suppose if you were a Buddhist, you're on the path that you're supposed to be on . . . that there was a reason for you to be prime minister, and it may be a reason you can't see.

SUCHOCKA: You know, I know a lot of very reasonable answers given me by [a] friend of mine, [by] different politicians, but it's not my own answer . . . I had to be convinced that it was really needed for me to be prime minister for the country, but now after 16 months . . . I'm not so convinced.

Mary Robinson, the president of Ireland, is also a law professor by background.

Q: You really didn't start out with the intention of having a political career.

ROBINSON: No, I didn't. I started with the intention of using my skills as a lawyer to influence . . . legislation, and to use law as a kind of instrument for social change.

Q: Would you say that women get involved in politics usually because of an issue, whereas men often seek politics as a career? And start their careers off that way?

ROBINSON: I think there may be a certain amount of broad truth in that, if I'm reflecting on the women that I would know both here in Ireland and elsewhere who have become involved. It's usually for a reason outside themselves that they want to change.

Norway's prime minister, Gro Harlem Brundtland, explained that the 'reason outside herself' in her case had to do with the issue of abortion. She spoke of the 'terrible dilemma ... of breaking off a pregnancy' and said that she 'felt very strongly how the law had to be made.' Her feelings led her to become very involved in Norway's abortion debate.

She then elaborated:

BRUNDTLAND: Well, you know when I was 35 ... the prime minister of this country surprised me very much by calling me to his office without saying why. I thought he was wishing to talk to me about the way to treat the abortion issue ... But then he said, 'I ask you to enter the cabinet,' and I was completely surprised ... I never planned to become a politician, although I always had a political interest, always was engaged in political debates and thinking; I never saw myself as a politician before I was asked to become one.

Maria Liberia-Peters is another woman who was invited in, as was Vigdis Finnbogadóttir, the president of Iceland, when friends and acquaintances pressed her to agree to run for her 'apolitical' post.

Q: Some people say that women get into politics because of an issue that's very important to them, maybe it's health care or child care or something like that. That men get into politics because it's a career. What do you think?

LIBERIA-PETERS: If I can say from my own experience, before getting actively involved in politics, I was very active in the social field. I'm a teacher, and in that way you were confronted with certain – let's say social problems – of your students, problems in family life, in the neighborhoods, certain needs and necessities of your students, which, at times, hinder them in making progress. And then, at a certain moment, from your position as teacher and educator, you start to become the ears, and the eyes and the feet of those who cannot walk, hear and see ... that's the way I walked right into politics. Because I was then approached at a certain moment in 1975 ... International Women's Year ... I was approached by the board of the political party to which I belonged, saying well, you know, why don't you get closer to the party, and why don't you get closer to politics, because it is through politics and getting involved, in being a member of the island council, being a commissioner, that's when you can really bring about changes. At first, I said, uh um, I think I can do my work best away from politics. Outside of the political arena. Until I decided, well, let's see what it's all about. And if I don't like it, I'll step out – that's what I thought. Until you realize that once you have stepped into politics, it's a one-way street.

Eugenia Charles of Dominica, a British-educated attorney, exemplifies a certain idealism which is typical of many of these women leaders.

CHARLES: We had had this march to present the petition on what you call the 'shut your mouth' bill. The leader of the country then ... came out and said that 'we are here to rule and rule we will.' And ... you know, that was the sentence that put me into politics. Before that, I was very loud-spoken. I felt I was a taxpayer and I had a right to express my view, I was paying for it! But I found that [his] reply was wrong. I mean 3,000 people had signed the petition, and that's a lot for Dominica, with its literacy, with its lower population, with a population that had been not very aware politically before, and I think that he could have at least said, 'We'll look at this petition, we'll see whether anything can be done about it. We don't offer any hope. But we'll at least consider it.' He could have said that much. But without reading it, without looking to see what the number of names were on it ... to say, 'we have to rule and rule we will.' I thought, 'Well, then, well then, we'll do everything we can to take you out of the ruling position.' It took us 10 years to do it.

Q: That was your defining moment?

CHARLES: That's when I decided that we had to be much further than just being concerned citizens.

My finding that a majority of the women presidents and prime ministers I interviewed came to politics 'by accident' or by invitation is not a new finding. It fits with other research on women who have played political roles, perhaps not at the *very* top, but during recent generations.[8]

Increasingly, however, women are not waiting to be asked to dance. They are putting aside hesitation, learning how their systems work, and – as did Margaret Thatcher – actively seeking out a political career. In my home state of Washington in 1992 nearly 100 women announced their candidacies for the state legislature,[9] and women ran for secretary of state, attorney general, insurance commissioner, land commissioner and justice of the state Supreme Court, as well as for the US Congress and the US Senate. Many of these women won: Patty Murray, a 'mom in tennis shoes', scored an upset victory to become one of Washington's two US senators.

The challenges these successful women faced were only just beginning, as the presidents and prime ministers I interviewed could have told them.

CHAPTER 3

Backgrounds

What you can pass on to your children is very, very important, and I say that to everybody who asks me about this.

VIOLETA CHAMORRO

The women leaders interviewed for this book have been willing to bear the heavy burden of governing and all come from backgrounds providing some of the resources needed for such a demanding effort.

Most come from well-off or professional families, some from families of very great wealth. (One exception is Margaret Thatcher.) A consequence of this is the opportunity for education. Many are highly educated indeed: they are attorneys or law professors (four); they hold doctorates in economics (two) or some other field of study (demography); one is a medical doctor; if from the Third World, they are likely to have studied in North America or England at some point in their lives. In some cases, their histories suggest that an academic career is a route into political power.

It may also be important that, in certain of their families, expectations were high for daughters as well as for sons. If we look, for example, at comments made by the prime minister of Norway, and by the presidents of Ireland and Iceland, we find this is the case.

BRUNDTLAND: The things they expected from me and from my brothers were the same. Of course, I was also the oldest child, but there was never any thinking that my younger brother, because he was a boy, would in any way be asked to do different things than I was being asked. We were just treated like equals from the beginning.

Mary Robinson spoke of how her parents – both doctors – encouraged all five children to develop their potential – and made her brothers do housework too (her brothers even 'claimed that I was the one who did less [housework] because I was the only girl'). Equal treatment was the standard in this 'very professional family'. Similarly, President Finnbogadóttir found that her father 'became a dedicated feminist when he had a daughter. Nothing was good enough for the daughter. And the daughter was absolutely capable of whatever my brother was capable of. Never a hesitation of that.'

When one thinks of the number of major cultures in the world where the birth of a daughter is still considered a disappointment (for example in India, Pakistan, China),[1] or at least much less desirable than having a son, the 'equality of expectation' in a few of these backgrounds is particularly striking. Benazir Bhutto, for instance, has said that 'Pakistan is a patriarchal society to the point of caricature';[2] she has also said that, because of her father's personal attitudes, there was 'no question'[3] that the opportunities available to her and her sisters would be good opportunities – equal to their brothers'. Bhutto's father went so far as to insist that his favourite daughter do graduate work at Oxford, one of his alma maters.

In England, Margaret Thatcher was very attached to her father, Alfred, who had no sons, but who also believed in a good education for his two daughters. To help Margaret qualify for Oxford, he paid for lessons in Latin and the classics.[4]

It has been written that, 'just as many forceful male political figures have had strong identification with their mothers (e.g., Lyndon Johnson), so too have most women leaders had very strong bonds to their fathers.'[5] However, without any prodding from me, several presidents and prime ministers brought up their mothers as important forces in their development. Lithuania's Kazimiera Prunskiene invited me to her home and opened her interview by introducing her mother in person. After her mother left us, Prunskiene commented:

I can't say that my childhood was easy. I was bereft of my father [at] one year old, and it was not easy for my mother to raise three children at the time. But as long as I remember her, she was always helping ... other people, and she was providing the best care for us. So, I consider that this is the teacher I took from my childhood and brought into ... [my adult] life. To take care of the other people, to work as much as possible ... My mother taught me to work without pressure, and this ability to work I brought into my present day life.

Hanna Suchocka of Poland also noted that her mother had taught her how to work hard. Her mother, a pharmacist, provided such a good example of a hard worker that 'I was well prepared for much work.'

Dominica and the Netherlands Antilles have strikingly different cultures from those of Lithuania and Poland, yet Caribbean leaders Eugenia Charles and Maria Liberia-Peters also spoke of the central position of their mothers in their lives.

CHARLES: It wasn't just my father. My mother was just as strong ... My *mother* was in control of the family. And *he* knew it. But it was because I had parents like *I* had that there was never *any* doubt in their minds that I was going to do the things I was to do, you know.

Liberia-Peters said that her mother 'had a very central position' in the lives of her five children: 'She really was the director.' Her mother's presence remains influential with her today:

My mother is 88 years of age, not very politically oriented, but the mere fact that I can go to my mother, she's a fat little lady, and rest my head on her chest and – just don't say anything, just keep silent – but just the fact that I can rest my head on her chest, gives me the strength to ... restore my confidence and go on ... God bless my mother.

It is clear from reading the literature on women's development that self-confidence or lack of it is a key issue. For example, the United Nations Institute for Training and Research (UNITAR) sponsored a workshop in the early 1980s 'to identify the obstacles that prevent women from participating in, and benefitting from, political life in their societies.'[6] The published report from the workshop said this:

Lack of confidence was identified as one of the major obstacles to women's greater participation in politics. A number of factors inspire, foster, or contribute to this lack of self-confidence. Numerous societal and familial pressures make most women feel that it is not legitimate for them to want more and more out of life, or actively to seek political change. Tradition and culture assign to women demanding roles within the small circles of family or immediate social groupings. Such demanding roles hinder women from gaining experience, and the accompanying self-confidence, outside their small circles.[7]

In the light of this it is interesting to note the extent to which President Vigdis Finnbogadóttir of Iceland saw her mother as a role model:

> I had a mother [who] never hesitated to take on responsibility, and I see ... now when I look back how very important it has been in my life. She was very engaged in everything, in social life in general, she was a nurse, head nurse in Iceland, an enthusiast dedicated to everything that she did, and I think that had much influence on my views, so to speak. I was against it as a child because I wanted to have mom at home, but later I see that, indeed, it has been a model.

Q: Can you give me an example of how you [are influenced], today?

FINNBOGADÓTTIR: Well ... responsibility is, of course, something that I find quite natural, and I wish that more women would not hesitate to shoulder responsibility. I think it's very important in the upbringing of every individual to teach ... about responsibility, because it is this hesitation – 'not me' – that has not always a good effect in society.

Q: What creates that hesitation for women?

FINNBOGADÓTTIR: Lack of self-confidence ... they all have to realize that this is something that women have to surmount; they cannot continue. We are not morally secure and that's our upbringing.

Q: We don't get that much reinforcement.

FINNBOGADÓTTIR: No. No. We worry about being judged. Whether it is in [a] large society or slower societies. Because we all live in onions. Onions, yes. You are the core of the onion and there are layers around you. And so – I don't know whether you are like that – they say we are afraid that those that we appreciate, in the layers in the onion, will judge us; say silly cow, what's she doing now? And you don't want to be called silly cow.

Eugenia Charles described why self-confidence is so important in governing:

> If you're not completely sure of yourself and you're not completely sure of what you're doing, the direction you're taking, you give up very quickly ... you have to know where you're going, you have to be sure of yourself, you have to be *completely* unconsumed with other people's opinion. And that sounds conceited – it isn't. It's just that if you want to be able to succeed, if you want to be able to carry out the projects you're thinking of, the *policies* you're thinking of, if you're wanting to do the things you think would help your country, you *have* to be able to be sure of yourself.

Some women expressed surprise at what they had – in fact – been able to do. Kazimiera Prunskiene said she was 'amazed', looking back, at the way in which she had been able to make decisions, despite having to deal with matters 'entirely unknown to me from my early experience'.

The development of a child's self-confidence begins at a very early age. Benazir Bhutto and Eugenia Charles emphasized the crucial influence the attitudes of their families had had on their upbringing.

BHUTTO: Well, I suppose that the single most important factor in my upbringing [was] a sense of *security* and a sense of *confidence* which my father gave to all his children, and even if I said something foolish, he gave it as much weight as though it were the most wonderful insight. I think this gives a child confidence and enables a child then to develop [a] thinking process.

Charles spoke of 'the whole spirit of the family where you sat down for meals together, and you argued, and you were never told as a child to shut up, you don't know what you're talking about. You're always allowed your opinion.'

Thirteen of the fifteen women in this book are themselves mothers (two of them via adoption – Maria Liberia-Peters and Vigdis

Finnbogadóttir). While their children have now mostly grown up, a few children (Benazir Bhutto's) are still very young, or teenagers (Maria Liberia-Peters'). I believe these heads of government or state would all agree: any parent who is raising children well – laying down a floor of self-confidence – is creating a potential for future leadership.

What else does it take to develop what researchers call a 'transformational' leader, one who truly seeks to alter a status quo? Both Gro Harlem Brundtland and Mary Robinson have been written about as 'transformational' feminist leaders.[8]

Prime Minister Brundtland described the kind of parental values – 'the basic thinking in my ... home' – which led to her career as a medical doctor and an eventual politician:

What I feel in my own upbringing and the atmosphere in my home was to try to do something which was meaningful outside of your own interests. You know ... how can you do something which ... makes a difference? How can you think to do something on behalf of others. This was the basic thinking in my own home, and I was reading the books of the early fights of the Social Democratic movement in this country, the physicians who went out and worked with people and did something, instead of being interested in their own income. People who made a difference in, on behalf of society. This kind of thinking and the right of every individual was always on my mind; it was not your own interests, but everybody's interests. This is the atmosphere in my own home, I would say. And I think this is what has to be there if you wish to move things ahead in your own society, and, more widely, in your own part of the world, or the world at large, which has been on my mind since I was small, in a sense.

President Robinson described conversations with her grandfather:

The influence I think that mattered in the sense of altruism was probably the influence of my grandfather, who was a solicitor ... he had to retire quite early on for ill health, and I used to talk to him a lot as a teenager,

12, 13, 14 ... he had a great sense of justice for the small person ... and the role of law in providing an opportunity for everyone to have their case heard. And he would give me examples, and the examples would generally be cases that he had either been involved in or had witnessed in the local courts. They were very local, small-town stories, but the underriding value there was, I think, promoting a sense of justice for the individual, no matter what the background of the individual – respect for everyone and the right of everyone to have access to the law and justice. It was quite an idealistic grounding, I think, and it certainly conditioned me in my approach to the law.

She also observed her father at work at his medical practice.

I saw his patients come and go – the elderly, the poor, the young. Nothing was too much trouble for him. He would talk about their problems, many of which were caused by strains and stresses outside the medical [arena], such as poor housing. He injected a very real sense of looking out into the community and being concerned about it.[9]

There is one further factor not to be overlooked in reviewing the leadership potential of these 15 women. With only two or three exceptions, they had seen relatives active in politics before them. They had watched fathers be ministers or mayors or provincial governors; they had seen grandfathers be senators; sometimes they had even seen a female relative active on the political scene. So while they might still have had everything to master concerning the particulars of governance or a specific position, they were like the duck who hatches near the pond and knows that this is water. Politics for them was not like something that happens on the moon.

And, certainly, when they themselves came into office, they learned that they were not on the moon, nor on a distant planet. As Tansu Ciller, prime minister of Turkey, put it, people 'put you under the microscope, and they're looking at you all the time. All the time.'

CHAPTER 4

Through a Different Lens

What I find amazing is that, when a man is designated as prime minister, nobody asks the French if they think it is a good thing that it is a man.

EDITH CRESSON

In a profile of Poland's Hanna Suchocka which he wrote for *The New York Times Magazine*,[1] journalist Stephen Engelberg tells this story:

> When Bronislaw Geremek, a leading member of the Polish Parliament, called to inform [President Lech] Walesa of Suchocka's selection as Prime Minister, the President was momentarily confounded. 'A woman?' he asked. There was silence on the line as he raced through the pros and cons in his head. 'A woman,' he said, his voice rising. 'Now *that's* smart.'

Engelberg goes on to explain that Walesa guessed that Poland's male-led parties would hesitate to intrigue against a female prime minister:

> Poland is a country in which men routinely kiss women's hands in greeting, and Polish men live by a rigorous unwritten code of what constitutes 'cultural' conduct. Many observers believe chivalry alone ... constrained Walesa from undermining Suchocka, as he has all other rivals from virtually the moment he became chairman of Solidarity in 1981.

Suchocka, when asked by Engelberg if being a woman was helping her govern, replied: 'I can't answer.' She then went on to say that 'my candidacy was accepted unexpectedly well, and ... with a lot of hope.' She added: 'This was most surprising and shocking.'

It is not unusual for a woman today to be seen as an asset in some political situations – particularly in circumstances where she is unexpected, or even a novelty, and can be shown to voters as a sign of a party's 'modernity' or renewal. Such motives came into play when Turkey's True Path party chose economist Tansu Ciller as party head and eventual prime minister. The choice of the stylish, Western-educated Ciller – who wears Chanel suits and generally shuns the traditional Muslim head scarf – could signal to voters and to the world that True Path was up-to-date and European-oriented, and that Turkey was not some Asian tribal backwater.

But once a woman is actually in office, focus quickly shifts from symbolic value to performance. And on no question posed to women at the top was there more uniformity of opinion than on this one: Are women leaders scrutinized differently than male leaders? From all quarters came a resounding Yes.

The fabric of response included the belief that people expect greater honesty from women, and that their publics sometimes have greater expectations that women can solve problems. Here, for example, is Khaleda Zia of Bangladesh:

Many people have great expectations from women leaders. They think that when a woman leader comes to power, many problems will be solved quickly and easily. But in countries like ours, I mean the developing and Third World countries, this is rather difficult.

Q: Would people go at you more, as a woman, than at a man?

AQUINO: Well, I think in my case that did happen, because here were the people under dictatorship for 20 years, and so, you cannot fault them for having such great expectations. And yet the reality is it'll be very difficult to undo or to change completely the wrongs that have been committed before you ... as I said, there were just too many great expectations.

Among these leaders there was the sense that women must try harder, work harder, than men – whether serving in a country of the developing or developed world.

LIBERIA-PETERS: I kept telling myself that my work was so important, and you had to put all into it, and everybody expected you to put everything into it, because nobody questions the [preparedness] of a man over [a] female, not even in my community, and I think over the whole world it's the same ... when you're a woman, you hear, oh, she's a kindergarten teacher, she's this, she's that and she's the other, and suddenly you are being questioned, so you have to put 100 percent, 200 percent in your work, you know.

Q: What do you think the standards are that people judge a leader by, the woman leader?

FINNBOGADÓTTIR: We all know that women have to do everything a little better than men. Women cannot afford to make [a] faux pas, as they say in French, that is quite clear. We're all so very, very tolerant when men make mistakes, but I don't know of any society that is tolerant when women make mistakes ... there's a tendency to say ... well, she's a woman. You'd never say, 'Well, he's a man, it's natural that he makes a mistake.' You do not say a thing. You only accept it.

The double burden which women carry in being both leaders and (typically) homemakers and mothers was addressed by Irish president Mary Robinson:

> If you take public and political life, women still have the main responsibility for family, child rearing, homemaking, and that's not shared in an equal and balanced way. And therefore there is that additional need, to be either more assertive, or better, or more determined, make more sacrifices, get up earlier, get to bed later, or whatever it may be.

Margaret Thatcher called herself 'dead lucky' that her husband's work was in London, her constituency was in London, Parliament met in London – 'everything just happened to gel' to make it possible to combine motherhood and politics.

Maria Liberia-Peters explained that children do not understand why a meeting is more important than an appointment that one has with them. She summed up the need to 'maintain an equilibrium between ... work and family life' by citing a Curaçao proverb: 'You cannot ... put on the lights in the street and keep your house in darkness.'

The question of a woman leader's female role – whether she is obliged to be married, or obliged to have children, to suit voter preferences – is now a complicated one that varies from culture to culture.

Benazir Bhutto has explained to interviewers that, in conservative
Pakistan, she could not function in politics without having a husband.

> I was under so much scrutiny. If my name had been linked with a man, it
> would have destroyed my political career. Actually, I had reconciled
> myself to a life without marriage or children for the sake of my career.
> And then my brothers got married. I realized I didn't even have a home,
> that in the future I couldn't do politics when I had to ask permission from
> their wives as to whether I could use the dining room or the telephone. I
> couldn't rent a home because a woman living on her own can be sus-
> pected of all kinds of scandalous associations. So keeping in mind that
> many people in Pakistan looked to me, I decided to make a personal sac-
> rifice in what I thought would be, more or less, a loveless marriage [her
> arranged marriage], a marriage of convenience.[2]

It has been pointed out that 'in the US political system, voters show
a clear preference for candidates with presentable spouses and one or
more children.'[3] In Washington State, in 1994, one of the male chal-
lengers to first-term Congresswoman Maria Cantwell repeatedly
asserted that her single status and lack of children implied human
failings of inner emptiness and over-aggressiveness. The gentleman
candidate touted himself as a more appropriate representative to
Congress because he was a family man with four children – an oddly
outdated position if one knows anything about population growth's
geometric progression and the disproportionate claim on world
resources of every child born in an advanced country.

Two unmarried leaders I interviewed could see advantages to their
single state.

CHARLES: It's harder for women who have families to take the flack,
because it spreads out to their husbands, to their children, and so I think
I'm fortunate to have so few relatives. I mean my parents are no longer
there to be annoyed by this, I haven't got any children who would suffer
because of criticism at school, 'look at what your mother is doing' . . . I

think it's easier, quite frankly. I'm not advocating that people in politics shouldn't get married and have families, mind you. I'm just saying that it's less of a burden if you don't have *that* to contend with as well.

No one expects a male politician to sacrifice marriage for the sake of his career. It would seem a very strange notion indeed. Yet related ideas have influenced the thinking of President Finnbogadóttir, because of cultural stereotypes affecting women.

> I'm not married, as you may know, and it is in a way my strength not to be married, because if I had been married, there would have been a great tendency to say: Her husband told her to say this. It was actually one of the elderly men, during the campaign 13 years ago, who pointed this out: 'I'm so happy that you're not married, because everybody would say that her husband told her [what] to say.' While a male candidate would never have been accused of being so under the influence of his wife that she was directing him. That is a fact.

Another lens which these women leaders have had to deal with is the media focus on female clothes and grooming, body parts and hair arrangements. While men occasionally encounter media reactions to their physical characteristics, such commentary is to be expected for women[4] – as Hanna Suchocka found out.

> I read such a lot of things in different newspapers on my ... personality, my clothes or my handbag, on my foulards. I never would read such a thing for men. It was all so very strange and difficult for me. For example, I like this colour you have – the jacket. I bought a jacket in this colour [hot pink] – I like it very much – and once I read in the newspapers: How is it possible for a prime minister to wear such a colour, such a jacket ... Why? Why is it not possible? I am first a woman, second I am prime minister. And so it is difficult.

Edith Cresson spoke of how 'cameras are not directed the same way if you are a woman ... For instance, when you get out of the car the cameras are focused on your legs. It never happens to a man'. Cresson went on to explain that there is a fundamental difference, 'in France in any case', in the media's approach to women and to men. With women, the media like to discuss 'the colour of her dress, the way she behaves, details linked to her as a person', rather than her politics or the measures she carries out.

Eugenia Charles, rather amusingly, described the method she uses to deal with male criticism.

> I really had a tough time, and they *tried* – it was really a baptismal fire. I mean they were trying everything to denigrate me as a *woman*. In fact, I couldn't allow it to happen because I didn't think along those lines. So ... I just said, 'Poor fellows, they don't know what they're talking about.' You know, that was the feeling I had about them. Commiserate with them in their ignorance in this respect. I didn't say it to them in those words. But in the back of my mind I was saying 'Poor fellows, they don't know what's happening,' you know.

Mary Robinson noted that it is not only men who react critically towards women in public life.

Q: Do you think women get scrutinized or reacted to differently than men do?

ROBINSON: Women in public life? Yes, I do, and part of that I think is other women. Scrutinizing, perhaps sometimes very critically, and that I suppose again is because there are fewer women, and they're under a different kind of challenge very often for that reason.

Edith Cresson pointed out that if anything should validate the competence of a woman in politics, it should be the fact that she convinced voters to elect her, perhaps over and over again. But often, she asserted, even repeated victories are not enough to establish one's right to have a role.

A woman who has a position similar to a man's must always be competent, but this is not only true in politics, it is true everywhere. The fact of her being competent will always be something that, by definition, people will have a tendency to deny her. I noticed that, not only regarding myself, but regarding a lot of women in ... French political life. People start with the idea of questioning her competence, whereas for a man they never do, by definition. If he was elected to such a position it is because he is competent. The only thing they cannot question are ... elections because after all we are elected people; that is to say that the people voted for us during the elections when we ran ... A man, who during the course of his life has never been elected anywhere, and who is named prime minister (it was the case with George Pompidou and Raymond Barre, who had never been elected to any position) – everyone found that absolutely normal. A woman who has been elected for 10 years at the National Assembly, at the 'Conseil General', that is to say at the regional level, who is the mayor of a city, it is as if she were coming out of nowhere. This is the big difference in the way men and women are treated.

In one or two countries, however, women leaders felt that the prejudiced treatment of women was changing, as women perform as heads of state or government. In Iceland there is said to be a body of children born since 1980 who think the president of Iceland is supposed to be a woman. And from Norway we hear this.

Q: Do you have a sense that there is any differing expectation or lens by which people evaluate a woman head of state or head of government?

BRUNDTLAND: Well, at least I am convinced that when I started in 1981 and became prime minister it was ... something that could be misused in the election campaign of that year against the Labour Party, which I was leading ... By playing on people's traditional feelings, cultural backgrounds, historical feelings. Because it was a new thing that a woman was prime minister, so, clearly, it was possible to play on subconscious, at least, feelings in people that – why is a woman at the helm? But in this country I think by all the years that have passed this has ... worn off. It is not so easy, I think, now to mobilize so many in that kind of negative sentiment, but it took many years, and I think we saw something of the same in the United States when Geraldine Ferraro was nominated for the vice presidency.

Q: But now, with your exceptional leadership, can you remove the fears that people have, or the misconceptions, perhaps?

BRUNDTLAND: I don't think there is much of that now, because people have confidence and have grown used to the fact that women can do the same leading work that men usually have done historically.

Let Benazir Bhutto have a last word on this subject:

Let's face it – women really started having careers since the sixties and seventies. Until then it was a very small number of women who worked, so the concept of the traditional ruler has undergone a dramatic change in the last 20 to 30 years. I think as the evolutionary process continues perhaps people will have a new idea of what the new traditions are, but until that occurs, you're still in the transition phase between one kind of society and another kind of society.

CHAPTER 5

Leadership Styles

*Women cannot lead without men, but men have
to this day considered themselves capable of
leading without women. Women would always
take men into consideration. That's the
difference.*

Vigdis Finnbogadóttir

Do men and women differ in leadership style? According to Michael Genovese, an academic who has studied the subject, some researchers believe so.

The difference in style has been spelled out in this way:

> Males use a hard style of leadership that stresses hierarchy, dominance and order. Women, on the other hand, exercise leadership characterized by a soft style of cooperation, influence and empowerment.[1]

A great deal of computer paper has been consumed in discussion of this highly controversial subject – and much more to discuss the role of gender in history.

Author Lawrence Stone wrote as follows when reviewing the five-volume *A History of Women in the West*:

> Is gender a useful category for historical analysis? It is certainly correct politically to argue that race, class and gender drive the machinery of history, and woe betide the historian who dares to question this formula, repeated in book after book like a mantra. And yet . . . a case may be made that gender played a much less independent role in the past than it is now fashionable to suppose. There is little doubt that life as it was experienced by a woman from a family of wealth and high status bore no relation whatsoever, before 1900, to life as it was experienced by a woman from an impoverished, menial family. Status and wealth were far more powerful controlling categories than gender.[2]

When the *Harvard Business Review* featured a debate on 'Ways Men and Women Lead', in its issue of January-February 1991, several researchers pointed out that a great many variables must be taken into account in comparing the behaviour of women and men in a particular circumstance or within a specific organization. Jane Mansbridge (Center for Urban Affairs and Policy Research, Evanston, Illinois) commented: 'Gender differences are fascinating, but they don't explain much of the variance between one manager and another.'[3]

What do the women interviewed for this book think about female and male leadership styles? Certainly they have all observed far more men in action as political leaders than they have women. But do they see a difference?

In a speech in Denver, Colorado, in 1992, Violeta Chamorro expressed firm views on the subject.

As you know, certain studies show that women traditionally lead by means of reconciliation, interrelations and persuasion, considering the fact that society has traditionally counted on the women to keep the family together, while men usually lead through control and intimidation. When women entered the fields of politics and business, they brought with them the moral values they had learned from home. These values have shown good results; I dare say they have even shown better results than did the traditional model created by men ... There are several ways in which men do not understand women. There is evidence of this everywhere. I think it is time that male leaders look to women leaders as role models. They will find that persuasion brings better results than confrontation. And, finally, they will realize that, when dealing with the nations of the world, reconciliation unites people and allows them to work together for the benefit of all.[4]

However, some women leaders offered other points of view. Hanna Suchocka was one. Suchocka has said that, in her former career as a law professor, she was surrounded almost exclusively by men.

Q: In your experience, from observing leadership styles, have you come to the conclusion that women have a different leadership style than men?

SUCHOCKA: No, you know, I didn't notice such a difference. And, for example, when I analyze the ... style of work of Margaret Thatcher, I see no difference.

The style Suchocka speaks of – she has a picture of Thatcher in her office – has been characterized as follows:

Thatcher was generally more ambitious, more of a centralizer, more autocratic, less collegial, more confrontational and more ideological than her predecessors.[5]

This biographer then adds: 'This assertive style was essential to her success. Not only did she take her cabinet and party by storm, she also took them by surprise. Thatcher was different, and the difference often worked.'[6]

The comment that Thatcher was 'different' – not simply from other women, but from previous British prime ministers, all of whom were male – makes one reflect on the role that expectation plays in leadership. How *much* can one differ, and within what contexts? Thatcher herself reported to me that she found no difference in style between the sexes, but a difference instead between 'someone who wants to be in politics and in power because they believe passionately in certain principles' and those whose motives are otherwise.

When I asked Kazimiera Prunskiene for her thinking on leadership, her initial response did not focus on any differences between men and women.

Q: You've met other world leaders, mostly men; what do you perceive about their leadership styles in comparison to yours, or perhaps to other women leaders?

PRUNSKIENE: Oh sure, I have met lots of the leaders of other states, both of Western states and of Eastern states. And they differed a lot. Mainly, due to different political systems that they were living in.

It was interesting, however, to see Prunskiene move on from this comment to assert that there are 'female' qualities that help women govern. Prunskiene said the following about her efforts to establish the independence of Lithuania from the Soviet Union during all of 1990.

I think that what helped a lot [was] being a woman. I was helped a lot in proving our independence, in establishing our independence, being a woman. Being a woman I found a new flexible way to convince the world. I found not such a straight and straightforward way to achieve our aims, which usually is very inherent to men.

Q: Tell me some more about that flexibility and those things that are inherent in women that men don't have.

PRUNSKIENE: I remember my communication, my dialogue, and it was not one-time dialogue but a continued dialogue, with the president of the [former] Soviet Union, Mr Gorbachev. I never [indicated that I was] underestimating him, I [indicated that I thought that he was very] important, I showed my understanding of his role even in our matters, but at the same time, trying to present *our* values and *our* understanding of the situation. Meanwhile there were certain forces who were inclined to present him as a tyrant, as the one who does damage to our nation. However, I thought that it's useless and even harmful to present him in such a light. I wanted to make him talk with us, to understand our position, and thus, with the help of the Western leaders, too, to achieve our aim.

What Prunskiene is talking about here is a psychological approach to another person which she identifies as a female approach. It involves acknowledging the significance of the other individual, trying to understand his or her position, and asking for understanding in turn ('I wanted to make him ... understand our position').

Maria Liberia-Peters similarly turned to a psychological context when asked to talk about leadership style.

I would not like to generalize, right, but leadership styles, the difference in leadership styles between women and men is – I think that as a woman I would prefer the consensus type of leadership. Why? Because, again, going back to my background, in psychology and in pedagogics, it is so that you get the best results when you convince the other partner, why we have to meet each other. The other style would be, that you say well, you know, I feel that this should happen and this is going to happen and I expect you all to let this all happen. But if you can convince people why they have to do certain things and why they have to go along with certain things, then their active participation can be longer lasting. And it could be also more; you stimulate . . . them to be more creative, also, in adding their little grain, you know, of sand to the finding of the solution. So I would continue to try to manage through the consensus style.

The release of energies which Liberia-Peters sees as an important result of consensus was also brought up by Irish President Mary Robinson.

Q: What have you observed as being the differences in leadership styles between men and women?

ROBINSON: I think there are broad differences, but it's quite hard to pin them down. I think women instinctively are less hierarchical, and I find that very much at the grassroots level in women's organizations and voluntary organizations here in Ireland that I keep very much in touch with. They're very open and enabling and participatory and they encourage each individual to have a role and an involvement. And I think it's the same when women are – generally – when women are in positions of leadership. It's not as hierarchical, it's not necessarily a question of asserting that a particular woman is an individual, as much as trying to influence others to come along a particular path, and trying to harness in a cooperative way the energies of those who are like-minded, whether it's a political party or in a professional group or whatever it may be.

Here's how Norway's Gro Harlem Brundtland responded when asked about women together in meetings:

Q: Do you ever sit back as you're in a cabinet meeting and look with perhaps amusement, or at least observe in a clinical way, that the women communicate differently than the men?

BRUNDTLAND: Yes, but you know, in a cabinet meeting itself, the communication is always between both men and women. But if you have a group of women sitting alone, it becomes more clear than when they are mixed with men ... women are more ready to use personal examples[7] and to couple their principle thinking or political thinking with concrete everyday observations in their own lives and in their neighbours' lives, and that makes the discussions sometimes more concretely based and more substantive, and it adds something to the totality of that discussion. If you don't understand the type of situation that a family in a local community is meeting everyday, then how can you sum up and have a total picture? Every person in a society is a detail, but the sum of all the details, or the sum of all the people, is how society functions.

Eugenia Charles came at the subject of *details* from a different angle, but one which she still identified as a female angle. Charles saw no difference between women making decisions and men making decisions, but she felt that 'women are inclined to ... look after the details more than men. Men have the grand vision, and they pass it on to somebody else to put into practice. Women follow the details more, they want to know that it *is* being put into practice.'

Q: Do you think that women could be open to the criticism of not having a grand vision?

CHARLES: No, I think that you have a grand vision. But you make sure that with a grand vision it is implemented. And men, I'm not saying that men don't do this, but they do this secondhand, through other people. And I think women ... keep their hand on the button all the time.

We have now had more than two decades of research on gender differences in politics, much of it done by Women's Studies scholars. State legislatures in the US have been one focus, since in some states women's representation in these bodies has reached the 20 to 30 percent range (or even higher). As with other research, the findings have varied according to how the analysis was conducted.

In a 1992 article in *The Chronicle of Higher Education*,[8] political scientist Lyn Kathlene from Purdue University argues that gender research must become more sophisticated, moving away from 'outcome' analysis – 'such as final votes or lists of what legislators think are top-priority issues' – towards examining 'how legislators conceptualize problems, what and whom they view as legitimate ... sources of information, and how they use their positions of power.'

In her own analysis of the 1989 Colorado House of Representatives, which was 33 percent female, Kathlene found that:

1) women thought differently from men about the origins of crime, and so proposed different kinds of crime bills

2) women's bills were more comprehensive and 'innovative' – and generated more opposition

3) men and women behaved differently as legislative committee chairs, with women acting more as facilitators and men more as controllers of hearings

4) men spoke up 'significantly earlier' in committee hearings, even when men and women legislators were equal in number on committee panels.

'Speaking up early' is sometimes a way of setting the agenda. Scholars have found it to be one of the ways in which Margaret Thatcher effectively exercised power:

> Thatcher possessed and expressed strong views, and she always completed her homework, which made her well prepared to argue her case. (Indeed, she often appeared better prepared than her cabinet colleagues.) Typically, she would voice her views at the start of cabinet meetings.[9]

Thus, 'Thatcher was quick to set the agenda and put her opponents at a disadvantage.'[10] And 'even when [she] failed to produce an agenda, her ministers sat in silence and waited for her to do so.'[11]

Scholar Patricia Lee Sykes has these words to say about Thatcher's 'different' style: 'The search for similarities among women as national leaders occurs in the context of fundamental contrasts between men and women, which places women in opposition as "the other". In a sense, failure to find hard-and-fast rules about women as ... leaders could ... signal success for those who appreciate diversity and seek to develop their own identities.'[12]

The Toughness Realm

On 3 December 1983, a small news item moved on the wires of Associated Press (AP), dateline San Francisco. It concerned a comment made by Charles Wick, then director of the United States Information Agency, to the newspaper publishers attending the winter meeting of the California Press Association.

Wick had been asked by a member of his audience why Margaret Thatcher opposed the US-led invasion of Grenada. According to AP, Wick replied that Thatcher's opposition 'was related to the fact that the British Prime Minister is a woman.' Wick then requested that his response not be put in print.

What makes this story so strange – and so amusing – is Wick's amnesia about Margaret Thatcher: only the year before, Prime Minister Thatcher's aggressive prosecution of the Malvinas/Falkland war had made her a hero to Britain's citizens and had greatly enhanced her political standing. According to one biographer: 'Almost overnight, her hold on power was solidified. Thatcher was now a world figure who [had] halted Britain's retreat [from Empire] and brought victory. Her popularity skyrocketed.[1] Wick chose to forget this history and instead fell back on stereotypes about women. He might have remembered that neither Golda Meir nor Indira Gandhi avoided being, in some phase, a warrior leader.

Issues of war and peace are complicated ones for women politicians. While a portion of their electorates wants to – and does – believe in the greater 'peaceableness' of women, another (often larger) segment is wary that women are not 'tough enough' to deal with military situations or defence concerns. Saddam Hussein's invasion of Kuwait, for example, setting off the Gulf War, is said to have hurt women's campaigns for office across the United States[2] – even though women fought in that war, and some came home in body bags.

Among the women leaders I interviewed, some felt, as did Vigdis Finnbogadóttir, that '*women in general* [my emphasis] are greater pacifists than men.'[3] The president of Iceland explained the difference by saying that women 'have this difficulty in facing death, premature death, and in facing wounded people.' However, her fuller response was more complicated:

Q: How about her role if a woman leader is also the chief of state, the head of the military, who has to deal with potential military conflict, how does she do that, do you think?

FINNBOGADÓTTIR: It depends, of course, how the woman is brought up. There are countries in this world that bring women in the military to fight, and it depends on the situation, and it depends on the mentality of the culture, of course. In my part of the world, in this part of the world, it seems to me impossible for women to fight, to carry arms, but, however, individuals are so different that way.

The same complexity of response came from Kazimiera Prunskiene:

PRUNSKIENE: In the younger days, the boys are usually playing war ... the girls are differently prepared for their lives ... I can hardly imagine a woman, a politician, who is seeking and escalating ... war.

Q: There's a belief by many people that a woman can't be tough enough to be in the top position because she would have trouble dealing with the military or going to war if necessary. What do you think about that?

PRUNSKIENE: I really think that women are more cautious in adopting such decisions. Surely they would seek for the other means which would enable them to avoid too sharp a conflict?

Then Prunskiene went on: 'But I don't think that the woman will ever sacrifice the interests of the nation or the interest of the state due to ... weakness.'

Both Sirimavo Bandaranaike and Corazon Aquino were forced to deal with – and did suppress – attempted military coups during their terms of office; Aquino found that, at first, her military command found it 'extremely difficult to accept a woman commander-in-chief.'

Violence, or the danger of military takeover, *at home* is more familiar to some women rulers of the Third World than it is to many male leaders of the developed countries. Khaleda Zia knows well the history of the military's role in Bangladesh, and it has been suggested that her government is helped by the fact that her assassinated husband was a professional soldier before he became an elected president. Sporadic political violence in Nicaragua and the Kurdish rebellion in Turkey have affected the governments of Violeta Chamorro and Tansu Ciller.

And then there is the case of Benazir Bhutto, who – accompanied by Prime Minister Ciller – made a special trip to Bosnia to show solidarity with victims of the Bosnian War. A journalist has described Bhutto's official aeroplane:

> In all the world there cannot be another plane quite like the official jet of the Prime Minister of Pakistan, Benazir Bhutto. The front section is a kind of office-cum-nursery, jammed with toys, briefcases, newspapers, nannies and Bhutto's children, Bilawal, 5, Bakhtawar, 4, and Asifa, 1. In the main cabin, political advisers, security commandos and generals are keeping an eye on the Prime Minister they cautiously support.
>
> 'Hello, gentlemen ... Hello, babies,' Bhutto calls as she enters the plane.
>
> It is both jarring and interesting to see soldiers saluting a woman with children on her lap.[4]

This light-hearted description belies the searing role that the military has played in the life of Pakistan and in the life of Benazir Bhutto. She saw her father deposed and hanged by a military regime, spent six years under house arrest or in prison, and saw her husband arrested when she filed to run for office in the October 1990 elections.

> It was a terrible time. Two officials came to tell me: 'Leave the country. If you leave, nothing will happen. But if you stay, your husband will be hanged and you will be disqualified [from holding office].' And I said, 'I won't go!' Later, some of them told me: 'You don't have to go abroad now, but don't file [nomination petitions for the October 1990 elections]. Your husband doesn't file and your mother doesn't file. If you do, your husband will be hanged and you will be disqualified and imprisoned.' Forty-eight hours after I filed, my husband was arrested.[5]

Because she really knows what it means to deal with the military, Bhutto talks tough on foreign and defence issues, and makes no secret of Pakistan's possession of nuclear bomb information – although in August of 1994, her government denied that Pakistan had already built a bomb. In Pakistani culture to talk any other way about these issues would be tantamount to surrendering a political role.

Bhutto, in the course of her life, has demonstrated so much personal bravery, so much real toughness, that it is rather ironic to hear her being accused of softness.

> I'm often told, don't be so soft. Be tougher. And I think that is perhaps the distinction between a male leader and a woman leader. I don't wish to sound like a female chauvinist, and I don't mean this as a disparaging remark on men, but just that – men often say to me that I should be more tough; they don't mean tough, they mean more ruthless. I can't just drop people. I've been accused of being too loyal, of accommodating people who were with me during the period of struggle, but I've always felt that people who did contribute so much of their lives for the restoration of democracy *must* be rewarded, so that if a democracy's under threat, more people can be inspired to fight for democracy.

Women politicians always face the 'personal toughness' issue, just as they always face the 'military toughness' issue: both are related to the way in which women are socialized. (US Senator Dianne Feinstein tried to cover herself when she picked as her 1990 campaign slogan: 'Tough, But Caring'.)

BHUTTO: I was taught that ladies try to have good manners.

Q: The opposite of that ... is the double edge – that nice is perceived as weak.

BHUTTO: Yes, and that's the problem, because being nice should *never* be perceived as being weak. It's not a sign of weakness, it's a sign of courtesy, manners, grace, a woman's ability to make everyone ... feel at home, and it should never be construed as weakness ... Men are comfortable with being intimidating; a woman is not comfortable with the thought that she is intimidating, and therefore, perhaps she tries to be a little informal, but that doesn't mean that the woman can't be tough when the time arises ... I believe that we should be nice to each other, and I tolerate a lot of nonsense because I like to be nice to people.

Corazon Aquino found that exercising executive authority and 'being a friend' can be a hard combination.

In the beginning ... when I had to fire a cabinet member, and where that cabinet member really was a friend – I found much difficulty there ... as time went on I realized that whatever emotions [you] may have ... towards a person, you have to set that aside, because, being president, you're not supposed to be guided by your feelings, but you just have to do what you believe is right, and what will be for the greater interest of the greater number.

Q: It's hard, though, isn't it, to keep your feelings down?

AQUINO: It is. It's something very different, and yet I guess I didn't completely lose all of my ... feminine feelings and ways, because people would tell me later on that when they wanted sympathy they could still go to me ... I couldn't definitely change totally – I mean, I am what I am, and maybe I could adjust and do some things differently, but I still continue to be very feminine, and I was not about to lose that kind of femininity.

In governing, Aquino also had to make adjustments to what she had been taught at school.

In school you're always taught to be polite, and you always ask – you don't command or you don't order. So, I remember, I guess in the first few months of my presidency, I would call in a cabinet member, or maybe a general or somebody working under me, and I would say, well, I would like to ask you to do this. And then, of course, I'm sure they were shocked. And then, later on, one of my advisors pointed it out to me, he said, 'Look, perhaps that was all right when you were not president, you know, to be polite and to ask instead of ordering.' So I think that is one of the first things, one of the first differences pointed out to me, where, I guess, as president, you're not expected to be polite, or you're not expected to be too concerned about good manners, etc.

Q: And probably, there might be the perception, that politeness was weakness.

AQUINO: Yes. I think that is it. You know, that you don't ask, you order. And so, well, I certainly learned that fast enough. But in the beginning . . . I guess from the time I went to school, and during my time, there was always what I refer to as an etiquette class. In fact one day, every week, in the school that I went to in New York, at high school, there was this lady would come to us, and the class was called Lessons in Charm and Good Manners, or something like that. We were taught how to sit and what to do in social engagements, which is, of course, so very different from what it is when you are president.

Q: They didn't teach you how to order generals?

AQUINO: No, they did not.

Two other women leaders – Hanna Suchocka and Mary Robinson – talked in their interviews about how the necessities of governing, or of simply getting involved in a political issue, had made them tougher women.

SUCHOCKA: I think that I changed a lot; for example, now, I can say that . . . I'm not so delicate . . . When somebody criticizes me I used to be upset for one, two hours . . . then I said, why? Because it was not a just comment . . . now when someone says I am stupid, I say – you are more stupid than me. It's my lesson . . . I changed really rapidly.

Mary Robinson explained that early on in her days in the Irish Senate, where she had worked to legalize contraceptives, she had encountered 'hatred at the popular level':

> I remember being very shocked and taken aback and deeply hurt, that I would get these kind of hate letters, and even have a sense that if people recognized me in the street that there could be a strong reaction, because I hadn't had that in my own background. And then I went through a kind of low period of suffering under that, and I came out strengthened, I think, by understanding that you pay a price for issues if you really believe in them. And I think I was glad I paid that price very early in my involvement in public life, because when you've paid it, somehow, next time it's a lot easier to stand up to criticism or conflict or public outcry.

President Robinson's willingness to be controversial – and to suffer for it – is certainly the best kind of example of genuine personal strength. One group of analysts of women's outcomes in the 1990 US elections found that 'the "toughness" a woman candidate needs to [demonstrate] ... need not be a military record, it can be any story of ... personal adversity overcome,'[6] and paths of altruism are certainly not excluded.

Three women writers have found that a 'tradition of principled, altruistic political service was forged by women throughout the nineteenth century'[7] in the United States – despite the fact that women could neither vote nor run for office. Accordingly, 'women typically sought to exert influence through moral persuasion and education rather than in the rough-and-tumble world inhabited by the male politician, with all its partisan manoeuvering. The male world might have been morally ambiguous and even corrupt – although not necessarily so – but it schooled its participants to compromise and deliver the goods. In short, while women were creating a political identity predicated on purity, men were learning to think of politics as the art of the possible and to practise compromise.'[8]

Practising compromise can itself be morally good or bad, depending, but the above analysis came to mind when I reviewed the answers that women leaders gave to this question: What in politics surprised you most? For what were you least prepared? Several answers displayed some discomfort with the political arena.

BRUNDTLAND: Well, I think ... in political life it is hard to live with the lack of integrity, the kind of infighting which is part of political life, because if you have entered this on an ideological basis, it becomes something that you dislike; some women will certainly be surprised at what they learn ... there were things happening around me that I felt [were] immoral and [that] should have been different.

CHARLES: I think that unfortunately women don't like the hurly burly of politics ... you don't get into being a leader in a country unless you go through the nasty role of politics. And it can be nasty. Oh, it's vicious.

PRUNSKIENE: Least of all I was prepared for the political game that usually goes on. I never expected it, and I had ... to understand [what was] going on ... even [when] I couldn't. When I came to power, I got into lots of behind the stage matters ... I feel that I had to know about the political games earlier.

FINNBOGADÓTTIR: I knew beforehand that there is competition in politics, and there is, let's say, negotiation ... other things are very much in the shadow – lobbying and things like that. The only thing I really dislike in politics is when, as we see sometimes, when there is dishonesty, even though it's all over the world. There is [a] kind of dishonesty linked to politics.

There are now opportunities for women in the United States and elsewhere to study leadership skills in workshops and classes, such as those sponsored by the Leadership Foundation Fellows programme. Such classes teach negotiating skills, the management of people, and strategic thinking, along with many other topics. The aspects of politics which these women presidents and prime ministers find disagreeable are certainly good case study subjects for potential leaders, if only as advance warning. As Maria Liberia-Peters stated: 'When you step in, you're very idealistic, you want to work for the benefit of the people and for the best interest of the people ... until sometimes you realize that there is more to it than just ... the interest of the people.'

CHAPTER 7

Heroes and Helpers

It is a somewhat ironic fact that, when asked to name their heroes, their important sources of inspiration, women leaders named mostly men. But the reason is not far to seek. As Prime Minister Brundtland explained:

> There are ... men in the picture because I did meet more men as a political leader than I met women ... that had more experience than myself, because I was one of the early women who took on the leading positions, and for that reason those I could learn from were men.

Brundtland was to name among her 'influences' Willy Brandt[1] and Olof Palme[2]:

> You know you stop having heroes when you get older. So now I would rather focus on what people have had an influence, made an impact on my own thinking, and then there are other politicians like Willy Brandt or, Olof Palme, because he was 10 years older than me and I could learn from him.

In her *childhood*, Brundtland said, Joan of Arc[3] and Golda Meir were heroes to her. Golda Meir was in fact the sole specific woman named by these prime ministers and presidents as a hero. Eugenia Charles selected her, and gave several reasons for admiring Meir, the former prime minister of Israel who took office in March of 1970 and died towards the end of the decade:

> She was so down-to-earth and practical. And she really made a lot of sacrifices for the country, you know. She really lost in the way of family life because of that, and that fortunately didn't happen to me.

In *Interview with History*, Oriana Fallaci reveals how Meir, if she invited a group of people to dinner, did all the cooking and cleaning up herself, even if it took the prime minister until 2 a.m. or 3 a.m., when she was in her seventies.

Sirimavo Bandaranaike – listing Marshal Tito[4] and Gamal Abdel Nasser[5] as among leaders she admires – gave the following explanation for admiring Nasser:

BANDARANAIKE: He was very kind. As you know, they had a revolution, but not a very bloody revolution. They didn't kill anybody.

In a not unrelated vein, Mary Robinson put famous apostles of non-violence on her list of influences.

I don't have obvious heroes. I have been influenced by some of the idealistic people: Gandhi,[6] Martin Luther King,[7] and Václav Havel[8] – they would be the kind of people – they all happen to be men – who would influence me because they are emphasizing very much important values for our time and for all time.

Edith Cresson added names of more men.

Q: Who has inspired you, who has been a model for you?

CRESSON: Like anybody else, I have had several models. I admired a lot of people, essentially people of character: De Gaulle,[9] Churchill,[10] François Mitterrand.[11] I also admired some people who are not well known, who were courageous in difficult circumstances ... I admired them for their character.

Q: Sometimes it is difficult for a well-known woman leader because there are not that many women leaders to admire in history.

CRESSON: Women only played a small part in history because we have only given them a small part to play. But there were some women who were admirable who, without having access to power, played a very important part in history ... Women played a very determining role during the Second World War especially, and despite this only De Gaulle had the idea of giving them the right to vote.

Women in France received the franchise only in 1944.

It is interesting that a number of women leaders spoke of deriving inspiration and psychological support from their collective citizenry – whom they often referred to as 'my people'. This terminology – 'my people' or 'the people' – is a very different language from that used by some US pundits, pollsters and politicians. Citizens of the US are not unaccustomed to hearing themselves described as 'the public', 'John Q. Public', or – most alienating of all – 'Joe Sixpack'. (Somehow one does not aspire to the equality of discourse of becoming 'Jill Sixpack'.)

For an instance of the identification between some of these women leaders and the people of their countries, here is how Corazon Aquino described her feelings when she realized what 'the People' were doing at one of her campaign rallies.

They were poor, and certainly they needed every single peso, and yet, they would be passing out this plastic pail. And at first I was wondering, what on earth are they doing? Here I was giving my speech, and I was seeing this plastic bucket being passed around and it was only later when I realized . . . they were dropping money there. Because, at the end of my speech, the leader of the barangay, the town where I was, would . . . present me with this bucket of money, and, you know, my heart really went out to them, because, I thought, if these people are willing to sacrifice for me, then certainly I should also be prepared, you know, to undergo whatever sacrifices are demanded of me. I think in a way it was the people who really inspired me to continue with this. Without them I don't think I would have dared challenge somebody as formidable as Mr Marcos.

Violeta Chamorro described a year of campaigning in similar terms:

I had a fractured leg, and I learned during that campaign how important it was to be with the people, to touch the people, to listen to them, and for that reason my own campaign was very easy as a result.

Maria Liberia-Peters discussed how important it was to feel close to her people:

> Talking, for instance, about security: I know security is, of course, very important, right? Because you have a very important job to do, a responsibility, you have to govern a country. I have children and they would like to see me grow very old. But I like to move around freely in the community. I don't like situations where, let's say, security officers keep me at a distance from the people, and that's why I participate ... in all kinds of folk activities, such as Carnival, such as neighbourhood parties ... Because my philosophy is, if the people have elected me, then when they're happy I should be happy with them, and when they're mourning I should mourn with them.

Benazir Bhutto said it was the confidence of her supporters that enabled her to go on, to 'face a very difficult odds', while Vigdis Finnbogadóttir spoke of her sense that 'my people are my friends'. Khaleda Zia asserted that she was not 'lonely at the top' because 'I am with my people, so I do not feel lonely.'

Of course these women leaders also turn to those closest to them personally for support and advice. A number mentioned one or more close relatives, a good friend, or a husband who was a source of help.

Q: And who do you turn to in that moment of loneliness at the top?

ROBINSON: I would turn in fact to my life partner Nick. One of the great riches I think about [our] marriage is [that] we were friends before we became more serious, and it's that friendship plus our relationship that is an enormous strength, and I draw on it quite a lot.

Benazir Bhutto has received criticism from some women because she agreed to an arranged marriage, which her critics considered an historically outdated method of taking a husband. Certainly this method has long traditions in both the Western and non-Western worlds.[12] Bhutto once had the following exchange with a *New York Times* reporter:

Q: At the time of your engagement, many women's rights advocates felt betrayed because they saw arranged marriages as part of the second-class status of women.

BHUTTO: Well, I don't agree with that. People today do computer dating. Is that a betrayal? When it's difficult to find a man, for whatever reason, one has to look for mediation.[13]

Bhutto then explained the role that her husband Asif plays in her life.

I feel there is someone to spoil me, to take care of me, comfort me. It's so nice to have somebody who cares about you. I was so lonely after my father died. I felt I was taking care of everybody else. With Asif, for once, I had somebody with whom I'd lay my hair on the pillow and feel I was safe.[14]

Women in the West may feel that their styles of living are light-years away from situations confronted by women today in the Third World, and in many cases they are. But a return to the history books soon reminds one of the similarities. We tend to forget, for example, how recently it has been that Western women achieved their legal rights, or even their right to an education equivalent to a man's. One historian has noted that, in Anglo-Saxon countries, 'women were denied control over their own property at marriage' until the late nineteenth century, and 'equal opportunity for women in the field of education is only about a century old.'[15] He commented:

In the long, sad history of women under patriarchy, nothing is more striking than their systematic deprivation of education, and it was this deprivation that robbed women of roles in the public sphere.[16]

CHAPTER 8

One Half of the World

In June of 1993 the *Los Angeles Times* published a special series of stories ('Women and Power') on women across the world.[1] The newspaper's reporters drew upon United Nations reports for statistics like these:

- Two-thirds of illiterate people in the developing world are women.

- As many as one hundred million women are 'missing' in the countries of the Third World – in other words, normal mortality patterns are not present. Female deaths during childbirth, infanticide and the 'nutritional neglect' of girl children are blamed.

- Thailand alone has 800,000 girl prostitutes under the age of sixteen.

For the 'advanced' industrial countries:

- Women hold jobs that make up 40 percent of total employment, but hold fewer than 10 percent of parliamentary seats, on average.

- One in five American women is likely to be a rape victim in her lifetime.

The leaders I interviewed are aware of the problems for women in their countries, whether the problem be sexism in France, reproductive freedom in Ireland, illiteracy in Bangladesh, or poverty in the Philippines. Today, many of these problems are increasingly seen not simply as difficulties causing suffering for individual women, but as restraints on national development. Human development, even more than the creation of a physical infrastructure of roads, say, or hydroelectric plants, is seen as key to national success, key to raised living standards. The prime minister of Bangladesh, Khaleda Zia, addressed this fact when she spoke as follows:

I can tell the women around the world, particularly from the angle of my new experience in my country, that women are still quite lagging much behind. Therefore, if the world is to develop and if the problems of different countries are to be solved, then women have to be given due importance, then women have to be valued and given recognition.

According to the United Nations, as recently as the early 1970s 'there were few indicators available ... to answer even the most basic questions'[2] about women's situations throughout the world. This changed, however, in 1991, when the UN published *The World's Women 1970–1990, Trends and Statistics*. Some of the information gathered was sobering indeed:

- 'In most countries in the developing regions, as well as in eastern Europe and the USSR, the economic outlook was far worse in 1990 than in 1970. And world-wide the population living in the poorest countries increased dramatically.'

- 'The number of illiterate women rose from 543 million in 1970 to 597 million in 1985, while the number of illiterate men rose from 348 million to 352 million.'

- 'Governments seldom integrate the concerns and interests of women into mainstream policies. Development policies typically emphasize export-oriented growth centered on cash crops, primary commodities and manufactures largely controlled by men. These policies typically neglect the informal sector and subsistence agriculture – the usual preserve of women.'

- Even today 'laws ... deny women equality with men in their rights to own land, borrow money and enter contracts. Even when women have de jure equality, the failures to carry out the law deny equality de facto.'

- 'Women still play a very minor role in high-level political and economic decision-making in most countries.'

The UN report could find a mere handful of nations with 'enough women in decision-making positions to have a strong influence.' The countries named were 'the Bahamas, Barbados, Dominica, Finland and Norway'. Dominica and Norway were, again, named as only three countries where women held 'more than 20 percent of ministerial-level government positions' – the other country was Bhutan.

Today women almost everywhere can vote, and they make up more than half of most electorates. Yet their share in the world's elected parliaments remains low, and has even dropped from fairly significant levels (around 25 percent) in Russia and Eastern Europe in the past few years.

The women I interviewed gave essentially four reasons why there should be more women in politics now. One was: it is women who really understand women's issues.

BANDARANAIKE: Yes. It is time for more women to step into parliament. We need more women.

Q: Why? Why should there be more women?

BANDARANAIKE: Because they are not considered. Women's problems are not considered now ... women have to work very hard, not necessarily at a desk in an office ... they have ... family problems that are different than what the men have.

The physical abuse of women which has now become a part of the human rights agenda across the world, with new groups monitoring the issue[3] and world conferences being held, was one women's issue specifically mentioned.

CHARLES: All the violence and abuse of women – I don't think it's a matter for women only to look after. I think that men are the ones [who] . . .
are the inflictors and therefore they're the ones who require correction.
But I think that women perhaps are taking different approaches to this
than . . . what men do.

A second reason given for needing more women in politics was the
sense these leaders had that women are better at understanding issues
of human support and welfare in general.

FINNBOGADÓTTIR: We in the Nordic countries . . . are very proud of the
fact that we have used the good economy in the country for the welfare
of the people. We have had such a splendid welfare system that it has
been . . . a model for the whole world that knows about it. We have also
gained very much in women's rights – for instance, there are more women
in the Nordic countries in government than anywhere else. However,
when there is a recession, where do they start cutting? They start cutting
at the welfare system, and that is where I think also women in decision-
making could be of very great use. Women understand how necessary it
is to have this welfare system, how necessary it is to have old people's
homes and hospitals, and they are very concerned about education – education is the key to everything, especially for them.

Some might be surprised to find Margaret Thatcher illustrating a
'woman's point-of-view' when she asserted that, while people are
'not entitled to be kept from the cradle to the grave by the government', they 'are entitled to a good education . . . because that gives
them the chance to develop their talents and abilities . . . also you
need a safety net of social services, because life is so specialized these
days, you can't have people in great need through no fault of their
own.'

PRUNSKIENE: I think that the feeling of care and responsibility for the children, for the aging parents, for the dearest ones ... all this transfers into the political life [of a woman]. Turning it into a cure for ... other people and turning it into care for the state.

Some leaders expressed – as yet a third reason for more power for women – their belief that women have a different (not necessarily a better) kind of awareness or intelligence than men.

FINNBOGADÓTTIR: There are nuances, differences in ... how women think and how men think, and that's quite natural because we are not completely alike ... we can put it ... that men can be grateful that they are as intelligent as women and women can be grateful that they are as intelligent as men. So there's no difference there. But the difference is physical and the approach is consequently different.

Mary Robinson saw this difference in awareness from the standpoint, in part, of the roles that women have had to play in the past.

Women speak from their experience and work outwards, and do so with increasing confidence as they find that what they are saying is at least as valid as what they're hearing from other sources. I do feel that women tend on the whole to draw more from their experience and to want to play a role in a power structure to influence change – it's part of a whole different reference point. Women in most contexts are coming from a kind of minority, if not marginalized, position into one where they're trying to move nearer the centre, and that brings with it all the empathy, the listening, and the sense of questioning, even ... whereas if you feel that the centre is your natural heritage, you may not be quite as open.

Finally, some leaders expressed a sense that elementary fairness ought to put women in power in some reasonable proportion to their numbers in a population. Vigdis Finnbogadóttir, Edith Cresson and Gro Harlem Brundtland stated that, since most populations are half female, women should be represented by their own. Prime Minister

Brundtland felt that this was necessary for the 'right decisions' to be made and for men and women to 'grow wiser together'.

So how do we come to this kind of integration, where women approximately equal men in cabinets or legislatures? In Norway – one of the few places where it has happened – I had the great pleasure of watching Prime Minister Brundtland's mixed cabinet gather together for the announcement of the names of that year's Nobel Prize winners. In place of the usual cabinet cluster of grey suits appeared *some* grey suits – and a lot of bright red dresses!

However, not all women leaders I interviewed were endorsers of the method that has been used in Norway to bring more women to parliament.

LIBERIA-PETERS: If I may say so, with all due respect, to situations where you have in certain countries, quota systems, there *must* be so many women in parliament, and there *must* be so many ... I don't believe in quota systems. I believe in trying to identify, because they are there, trying to identify women who can do the job, who can do certain jobs, and give them confidence, give them confidence so that they can do it.

Margaret Thatcher stated that she was 'very much against ... having a quota of women. It's totally and utterly wrong. In my life it's merit and suitability that count.'

Hanna Suchocka, remembering days when Communist parliaments reflected Marxism's espousal of 'equality of all citizens regardless of sex', offered this:

I remember women being in parliament in Communist times. Sometimes I was of the opinion ... that women didn't know [why they were] here in the building. Because they didn't understand what ... work in parliament [is]. Because they [found] themselves in parliament only because [of] numerous clauses for different political parties ... it was written that from this and this constituency it must be women ... the women in parliament now ... are really active women. And, of course, they very often have different opinions than I have, but they are active, they know how to argue. I think that the problem is not only the number of women, but . . . the quality of women . . . in parliament and politics.

While the issue of quotas – wherever raised – always seems to arouse differences of opinion, their success in Norway has depended upon certain features of the Norwegian electoral system. The country – like most continental European nations[4] – uses a proportional system of voting in which parties (there are several, not simply two) run their proposed parliamentary (or municipal council) candidates in groups (lists) in each jurisdiction. Each party that achieves a certain number of votes will get some representation, and the names of candidates at the top of the lists will be taken first, to serve. This is in contrast to an electoral system like that in the United States, in which candidates run as individuals, each of the two major parties eventually sponsors a candidate, and one major party winner emerging in each contest, regardless of how close the vote was.

Proportional voting systems give women (or minorities) a better chance to be represented; they also involve more coalition building, since more parties (views) are represented in an elected body. In Norway, the parties of the centre and the left now reserve quotas on their lists for women. The big breakthrough came in 1983, when the Labour Party, led (not incidentally) by Gro Harlem Brundtland, adopted a 40-percent-women quota for all of its lists.

This achievement did not come out of the blue. Agitation for more women on party lists began in the late 1960s – prior to that time Norway's parliament of about 150 members had a less than 10 per-cent representation of women, no better than most countries today. Continual work by women's organizations led to this situation in 1983. This is the larger story of Norway's success, beyond the par-ticular features of its electoral system.

One academic researcher who has studied Norway is Jill M Bystydzienski, a member of the faculty at Franklin College in Indiana. Her research in 1986 'indicated that women in public offices in Norway contributed to a change in the political agenda and to the climate in government . . . Once a significant number of women (filling at least 15 percent of the total number of positions) found their way into government, they began to raise women's issues and concerns.'[5] They also made it possible for politicians in general to behave differently:

> Whereas fifteen years ago it would have been unheard of for a minister to excuse himself from a meeting because he had to pick up his child from a nursery school, today such an occurrence hardly raises an eyebrow.[6]

However, Bystydzienski has sounded two cautions about these significant changes, one concerning Norway and one concerning reform in general:

1) 'In addition to economic problems faced by the country, which have led to increasing conservatism and limited experimentation, the structures within which . . . women must operate are well-entrenched and still largely male-dominated.'[7]

2) The strategies pursued by women in Norway, 'where access to public offices is relatively open and official ideologies espouse "equality"'[8] may not work elsewhere. Societies less open may require other tactics to give people – and not simply women – more access. The president of Ireland, Mary Robinson, showed her awareness of the need to think through each national situation:

> I believe there are various ways in which countries will address these things, discussing issues such as quotas, role models, ways of encouraging, and I think it will be different combinations . . . depending on different countries. I also think that conferences such as the forthcoming Beijing Conference are very important taking-stock opportunities. It is important to have a whole process of taking stock.

The Beijing Conference to which President Robinson refers, taking place in China in September of 1995, is the fourth international conference on women which the United Nations has held – others took place in 1975, 1980, and 1985, in Mexico City, Copenhagen, and Nairobi. The 'final brochure' for the Beijing conference notes that 'only seven of the 184 Ambassadors to the United Nations are women. Only four of the UN specialized agencies and programmes are headed by women.' The leaders I interviewed called for more women in high positions at the UN.

Q: What role should women be playing in the United Nations that they are not yet performing, in your mind?

PRUNSKIENE: Well, I think, as far as I know . . . all the different missions conducted by the United Nations are being led by men exclusively up until the present moment, and I think that this is not good, if we are taught about the development of democracy in the world, because you cannot talk about . . . democracy as such if you are using only one half of . . . humanity.

While Benazir Bhutto was able to point out that her own mother was active at the UN representing Pakistan and the Commission on the issue of Women's Rights, there was a perception that women are under-represented.

Q: Let's turn to the UN for a little while. What role do you think women can – could – play in the UN that they're not playing yet, and what would be the benefit of that?

LIBERIA-PETERS: Yeah, I really wonder, I really wonder at times why an organization such as the United Nations, that found it necessary to proclaim a decade to stimulate [the] participation of women, [in] all fields of life, [in] all aspects of life, still in their organization has not yet been able to physically give that example. I find that it is still very much a man's organization.

In fairness to the UN, Prime Minister Brundtland pointed out that the problem of inadequate female representation has not gone unrecognized in important quarters there. She noted that 'the secretary-general, of course, has made that an issue and is trying to pursue this.'

Mary Robinson called attention to the way in which non-governmental organizations (NGOs) – particularly networks of women's groups – can try to influence and support the work of the UN.

Q: Perhaps we should consider the UN to be precisely one of those models that should include more women.

ROBINSON: Yes, and perhaps be influenced by the kinds of structures that are evolved by women, for example, the capacity to network, the capacity to link an informal grouping together in very supporting and helpful ways. I think that this way of networking and networking between networks and networking in a way that links grassroots organizations into systems, is very important. And I'm glad that the role of non-governmental organizations is becoming increasingly important.

Sirimavo Bandaranaike acknowledged that not all women are awake to the role they can play – a fact certainly not unrelated to private difficulties.

Q: The country has much to be proud of – high literacy rates, high health rates. What more would you like to see for women in Sri Lanka?

BANDARANAIKE: Women taking a more important place in the country, in the interest of the country. I'm sorry to say most women are not interested in what's happening in the country. They think of their families and themselves, but not enough [of] what's happening in their country. They assume only the men in government can play with the important part.

Q: Why?

BANDARANAIKE: Well ... they've never been interested.

Q: How do you get them interested?

BANDARANAIKE: We have to do a little propaganda . . . we have to wake them up.

Q: How can more women come into power?

BANDARANAIKE: Well . . . when people work, they can come into power.

CHAPTER 9

A Handbook of Advice

*Question: What advice will you give to the
future prime ministers of the world?
Well, they must keep in touch with world leaders and know what's happening in the world.*

SIRIMAVO BANDARANAIKE

The women interviewed for this book represent a rich bank of political experience. It seemed fitting to ask them for the advice they would give – not only to future women leading at the top – but to any woman planning to enter politics.

Their judgements and suggestions ranged over a wide variety of topics, and were sometimes funny, occasionally tinged with bitterness, most often simply serious.

Q: What advice would you give to a woman who wants to go into politics now?

CRESSON: Well, it depends at which level, of course. If a young woman goes into politics, first she has to join a project. Meaning you do not do politics as you do accounting, for instance, or anything like it. She has to join a project, to formulate or have contributed to formulate this project . . . to want and to agree to sacrifice a lot of things for this project. So I will advise her not to get involved if she does not believe in it.

Margaret Thatcher's advice was not dissimilar:

Come into politics . . . because you believe in certain things. That's the only reason for coming in.

Eugenia Charles offered more on being serious.

Q: So what do you say to young women?

CHARLES: I think they must *know* – they must know their minds. You can't do anything half-hearted in this world. You must know what you *want*. You must know, also *appreciate*, that this is what will do to bring out the results, the goal, that you're looking for. And then you must look for the right way to do it and follow it. And not let *anybody else* interfere with it.

Hanna Suchocka, having served in different capacities, pointed at the difference between being a member of a parliament and acting as a nation's chief executive:

> I [had] not been prepared for being prime minister totally; I was a member of parliament, but it is quite different to be . . . prime minister.

Suchocka, as a law professor, was used to studying her issues in a particular way.

> Suddenly I found myself in the position of a person who must know everything . . . And it was really difficult because I was a professional being in the university . . . and suddenly I noticed I had to undertake particular decisions without the ability to study or documents . . . I felt that one of the first things I had to do was to find a group of advisers, because without advisers it's impossible to be prime minister.

Edith Cresson stressed the importance of being able to choose advisers whom one knows extremely well – if one can.

Q: How does one know, determine whom to trust, as advisers, as ministers, in a leadership situation?

CRESSON: I think that choosing one's advisers, one's ministers, is one of the most difficult things. You have to know that you are not entirely free to choose the ministers (far from it). As far as I [was] concerned, my freedom was certainly limited. Indeed, it is very important to select advisers and ministers, and one must and should stick to people that one has [known] for a long time. (I was able to do so in some occasions); one must also select people one trusts because one knows that they are devoted to the general interest of the country and do not pursue their self-interest. Once again, one does not always have the possibility to choose, but if one does, these are the people that must be selected.

Corazon Aquino spoke very frankly of the difficulty she had in choosing the right people for her cabinet.

Q: We all learn from our experiences so that, if you could go back knowing what you know now, and start back again, how would you have done it differently?

AQUINO: Well, I guess in the choice of cabinet members. Before becoming president ... I was being, well, lambasted by Mr Marcos saying, how can you elect a housewife who knows nothing about running a government? To which I said, yes, it is true, I do not have the experience that he has ... I'm not experienced in cheating, lying, etc. However ... I felt confident then that I would be able to get 15 men and women to help me. And many [said] that this would constitute the nucleus of government activities. Well, I thought that the main qualities that I should look for were honesty and competence in government officials. I did not know until later how necessary it was to have a third quality, and that is the ability to work well with others. I mean, you can have a cabinet full of stars, and really the most brilliant people, but if these people cannot relate to each other, or if they cannot be humble enough to accept that perhaps somebody else has a better way of doing it, then you are in trouble. So, if I had to do it all over again, I would look for men and women who have that ability to work well with others, because it's only in that way that you will be able to effectively carry out the government's programmes. Honesty and competence, of course, are two very desirable qualities, but the third quality of cooperating and working with others is also an absolute necessity.

Kazimiera Prunskiene also noted the trouble she had, early on in her career, putting together her 'team'.

Q: How do you decide whom you can trust?

PRUNSKIENE: It's very difficult to answer such a question, and I think you cannot avoid making mistakes. And also, I made mistakes in relying [on] and trusting ... other people, in trusting those whom I invited to take part in my team. But I would say that with experience you learn somehow, and intuition helps you a lot. To see the person and to know that he's the one you can rely on. You see the other person and you find something strange about that person and you know immediately that you cannot trust or rely on such [a] person ... At the very beginning of my political career, it was very difficult for me to choose the people who would comprise my team ... Now, when I look back, and with all the experience, I think it would be much easier for me to do that.

Of all the women I interviewed, Edith Cresson and Benazir Bhutto seemed to be particularly conscious of the power of the media. Cresson urged that a newcomer to politics should have members of her team who know how to work with journalists:

I will advise her to try to form around her a very serious protection made of people who know well the media and who are ready to spend a lot of time with the journalists to explain what she does or what she wants to do, to get surrounded by a certain number of women, and I will advise her not to work constantly, but also to polish the image she wants to give of herself, and to polish it by frequent encounters with political journalists.

Cresson issued the following assessment and warning:

The game is not what people may think it is at first. And there is also a very big distortion of democracy which is amplified by television through the constant speeches given, not by politicians, but by the ones who comment on politicians; and the true power is in fact in the hands of these people. Someone who is in politics or someone who achieves something thinks that he has to fight against his political opponents, but in fact he has to fight against professional people who do not have to question themselves, who do not take any risks, who are never penalized, who therefore get what is the closest to absolute power.

Benazir Bhutto proffered a similar analysis.

> In fact, I think that we are on the threshold of a whole new world; the previous world [was an] industrial age ... But now we are [part of] of the information age, when images from one part of the world can so quickly and rapidly be transported to another part of the world. Ninety percent of the people believe what they see, so it's going to be information and the people who are in information who are going to be the real leaders of power and influence the shape of society.

She continued:

> The media follows stories which interest it; not all stories are considered interesting, and usually those stories are considered interesting which are scandalous or which are not good ... So in the past, while we taught our children – at least I as a child when I was growing up was taught about heroes and historical figures or even contemporary figures who would inspire one forward – today there ... seems to be a [reversal] of that rule; an attempt is made to scrutinize and analyze to such an extent that one is not looking for the good qualities in a person; that's not news, goody goody is not news. But scandal is. Ninety percent of the people are not reported. It's only 10 percent of the people who are reported so ... 90 percent view the remaining 10 percent. And we very much depend on it, on the media people, and that's why I see a shift of power towards those who are in the world of journalism, television, media and the entertainment world.

However powerful it may be, the media is only one ingredient in the complex mix which must be dealt with by a leader. Corazon Aquino spoke of the need to hear out the views of all of the institutions and persons who are a part of a particular situation.

> As president of a democracy, you have to contend not only with the legislature, and also the power of the judiciary, but we have these other sectors like, well, the environmentalist and other organizations ... which

you would have to contend with, and it's not as if you can just dismiss their concerns. I mean you really have to talk with them, to have a dialogue with them and find out how their perceived concerns can be addressed, and how both of you could be working together.

After all the dialogue, Maria Liberia-Peters pointed out, comes the moment when a leader does what she's there for.

LIBERIA-PETERS: One advantage of consensus is that you can get a broader participation. But you have to know when the moment has been reached to say well, OK, now I have to assume my responsibility. Because if you don't know, if you lose the momentum of assuming your responsibility, then, you know, everything can be lost. Even sometimes when assuming the responsibility, you know that you are going to face a very difficult situation. I have had difficult situations of general strikes in the community where you go on talking with all the various interest groups in the community, you talk to the business world, you talk to the unions, you talk to the church groups, the women's groups, to all kinds of groups, and say, listen, this is what has to happen ... But what comes out is that everybody realizes what has to happen, but when it comes down to unpopular measures, everybody lets you feel it's your responsibility. So then you have to assume your responsibility, come what may. So consensus, yes. But know when to assume your responsibility and take the decision that you feel you have to take.

Hopefully, decisions are made in the context of some overall sense of direction. Benazir Bhutto put it like this:

I believe the most important thing is not to lose the perspective of where one is heading. To me the most important aspect of my own government, my first term and second, has been economic management.

She cautioned:

One must be flexible to survive in politics, not rigid, not dogmatic. Yet one must not abandon one's principles, so I would say that flexibility within a framework of one's beliefs and values [is basic].

Leadership may also involve finding new, innovating ways to communicate. Mary Robinson, when elected president of Ireland, faced the problem of holding an office that did not initiate policy or advocate new laws.

I've had to change the style and method of communication because the office of president of Ireland is not an executive, policy-making, or legislative-initiating office, and so I have to use the language of symbols, and think of lateral ways of communicating, and of encouraging trends in society without being directly involved in policy making. It's very interesting.

Robinson further explained her search for the 'language of symbols'.

In the inaugural address, I was trying to envisage the various ways in which I might seek to address an influence. And I remember that I said that I would wish to play a humanitarian role on behalf of the Irish people, because this is a small democracy with its own past history, which can give it an empathy and a closeness linked to developing countries. But in saying that I would like to play a humanitarian role, I had no idea, I had really no idea. I remember saying to myself, what could I do, as a non-executive president?

In fact, it has been possible to play that role in practice, for example, visiting Somalia and being general rapporteur of an inter-regional human rights meeting in Salzburg last January, and in other, smaller ways. But I remember agonizing over how specifically it would happen, and I think it has been true in a lot of other areas. I wanted to link with the extended Irish family around the world; how do you link? You start, apparently, as I learned, with a very modest emblem, a light here in the window of my residence. And by placing that light physically in the window, where it can be seen from the public road, going through the park, and then referring to it – there will always be a light in the window [of the presidential residence for the people of the Irish diaspora] – I have somehow focused on a symbol that has travelled all around the world. And when I go to Australia, when I go to New Zealand, the Irish community there knows about that light. So, it's very interesting to recognize the power and potency and communication that there can be through symbols, through language, that touches on values, rather than specifics, of immediate policy.

Finally – in leadership, there is always room for humour – and room for silence.

LIBERIA-PETERS: I started out in 1962 as an early childhood educator. OK, you [govern] with psychology and keep meeting; there is basically no difference in the behaviour of a four, five, six-year old or a forty, fifty, or sixty-year old. Basically no difference. And I keep telling them that in the meeting of the Council of Ministers.

Q: Still need to pat them on the head, give them cookies and milk?

LIBERIA-PETERS: No difference.

AQUINO: What . . . I learned was not to give unsolicited advice – just keep quiet.

CHAPTER 10

Reflections on Women's Leadership

Let us go back for a moment. What are the reasons articulated for having women leaders?

Simple and basic: women have different points of view, values, experiences, priorities, interests and conditions of life. Theirs are not necessarily better, more noble, more important, but they are theirs.

Any issue carries different prisms, depending upon one's personal worldview. Cuts for kindergartens may mean something different for men than for women. A man may rely upon child-care, but just not know it in the same way that a woman might.

If a man takes care of the household finances, he may be aware of and concerned about the capital gains tax and its impact. If a woman works in a low-wage job, she may focus more clearly on workplace problems.

A man can understand and empathize with the woman who tells of her fear to walk outside at night, but he needs to experience the threat, and may not ever be able to do so. During law school, a professor of mine related a story of how Supreme Court justices, dealing with an issue of personal security, were unable to understand what a woman felt during a purse snatching and mugging. Only the one woman then on the Supreme Court understood.

Men and women can walk in one another's shoes only partially – the rest is either imagined or not considered at all.

So women must be able to represent themselves.

None of us escapes our background, sex, class, race.

This is, of course, true for the women leaders in this book.

Despite their similarities, they are not all alike. They hold different religious beliefs, different political beliefs, different orientations towards their still-unique roles as woman leaders. While they are the largest simultaneous group of modern presidents and prime ministers the world has seen to date, most of them have not functioned in an environment where they were surrounded and supported by many other women.

According to Drude Dahlerup, a European political scientist, three conditions are crucial for women leaders if they are to strongly support (assuming they wish to do so) the kind of feminist agenda that would be relevant in any country, namely, an agenda which ensures women's personal safety and security, provides the ability to plan and control childbirth, equalizes access to government and free-market resources, and can change political and legal rules to give women true equality with men.

The first of Dahlerup's three conditions is that there must be a large number of women inside political institutions. Second, there must be well-organized, strong, active women's organizations to both support and criticize women (and men) politicians, and to act as experts in assisting on issues of importance. Third, there must be continuing sources of 'outside' energy to continue to challenge any 'Establishment' with new and more flinty visions. The latter two conditions are those that also help put more women *into* political institutions, condition number one.

More than one of these leaders came to power not in some ordered, evolutionary fashion connected with the conditions Dahlerup proposes, but before the 'natural time' when one would expect such leaders to emerge. They came as anomalies to women's development, like wild flowers growing because of rare genetic mutation. Because of lack of a full supporting structure, the advances they can make for women may come in flickers – perhaps, for example, appointing other women to cabinet posts or judgeships, or to posts where their appointees can in turn appoint other women down the line.

To do even this much may require overcoming not only external forces, but internal resistances. A woman leader may, paradoxically, carry some of the same prejudices and stereotypes put upon her gender by others. Or she may strongly believe that it is up to the individual – female or male – to make their way in the world, independent, self-responsible, not looking to government to in any way assist or even out a playing field. Religious beliefs may affect her attitude towards reproductive freedom, which will in turn affect major issues like her country's population demands. A woman leader may sense that her mandate is severely limited, and that it is far too risky to extend herself into new territory or to take on the agenda that really represents her own unique perspective. Her party or her advisers may be strongly against her doing so. And once in office, it is a rare leader who does not want to maintain and enlarge a power base. Ignoring more radical women who are making demands may be one way of doing so.

Of course the external constraints are endless. In countries like the United States, where huge amounts of money are legally poured into electoral races to maintain the power of all kinds of special interests, financial hurdles may keep a woman from challenging an incumbent to begin with. The power of money and the power of incumbency are such that, although voters decry those currently in elected office, they generally vote them back in at a ratio of about 9:1 in the US. This in a system where key leadership and committee chair positions are largely male territories.

How individuals get elected in a particular nation can substantially lessen or increase opportunities for women. Almost all countries in the United Nations which call themselves democracies enjoy some form of proportional representation in voting – exceptions being the United States, Canada and Great Britain.

Proportional voting puts lists of candidates in front of the voters by parties. It is quickly obvious if a party list includes many, if any, women. A clear picture speeds the ability to demand quotas or other forms of demonstrable representation. Proportional voting also gives voters a wider choice of political views and parties, and, although it creates less stable governments and leads to more elections, it does open the gates for parties that have small but active constituents (such as the women's party in Iceland, or various Green parties).

When the head of the party which wins an election automatically becomes the prime minister, it is easier for a woman to become head of government. In this kind of system, unlike that in the United States, voters do not choose a chief executive directly. Instead, they elect their representatives to parliament, and the leader of the party with the most representatives becomes prime minister. Those who put themselves forth to head a party are known to other party members through party meetings, actions on the floor and other kinds of close interaction. In the much more diffuse US system of naming a president, where parties count for less and less, and candidates must try to mobilize the electorate in state after state, the top leader who finally emerges is now likely to be the end product of television ads and a handful of 'presidential debates'.

What are the other factors that keep women out? Depending on the nation involved, the answer may involve cultural norms, religious beliefs, economic demands, educational opportunities, and a host of other factors that are part of a country's history, apart from the explicit mechanics of its electoral process. The first step for women in seeking fuller representation will be to analyze their own specific barriers to greater power. As can be seen from some of the country histories which appear later in this book, what has counted for women historically is to organize, organize, and then organize some more.

Various studies have indicated that, to make a difference, women must reach a 'critical mass' in political institutions. The number necessary for the critical mass has been found to vary. The United Nations Division for the Advancement of Women did studies in 1987, 1990 and 1994, and found that a 30 percent representation was the number necessary. Not to make a revolution, but to make a difference. However, revolutions are made one step at a time. Critical to a revolution for women will be the media, as Edith Cresson and Benazir Bhutto noted in their interviews. If the print media, talk shows and other outlets do not cover women's 'political' activities, broadly defined, it will be up to women to demand that they do so.

Whatever the limitations of today's media coverage, it has the ability to spread images, like pollen, around the world. The BBC, *The Times*, CNN, *USA Today* and other outlets all carry pictures at times of women leaders, and these pictures help remove, pebble by pebble, the stone wall which surrounds the definition of who women are and what they can accomplish. *Vive la femme*.

CHAPTER 11

Geography and Gender

*Note: The reader should consult **Country Notes** concerning the reference system used in this chapter.*

BANGLADESH

In Bangladesh, women are subordinate, second-class citizens by virtue of historical and religious tradition. Sons are valued as the sex that provides for parents in old age; girls have traditionally been less educated and have even been fed less food – a deprivation reflected in the fact that women are less than half the population of Bangladesh. Because a woman must customarily bring a dowry to her husband's family when she marries, and takes her capacity for work away from her own family, a saying in the country goes that spending money on a girl child means 'planting trees for other people's gardens'.

Bangladesh, with its large population of 120 million, is an overwhelmingly agricultural society. Women's rural labour has been needed to help families survive. Women still hold only a small fraction of wage-earning jobs in the country; the garment industry is one area where they are concentrated. Fewer than 5 percent of government jobs are held by women, despite a government goal of 15 percent.

Given Bangladesh's great poverty and its anti-female traditions, it is interesting that the country has recently had about the same percentage of women in the legislature as Britain has in the House of Commons – around 10 percent. However, that figure has been lower in the recent past. Bangladesh has reserved some parliamentary seats for women only. However, the number is so small (30 of over 300 seats) that 'women's seats' have served as a token to enable parties to avoid having more women candidates on regular party slates. Much press reporting has been generated by the fact that two major parties are led by women – one of them Prime Minister Zia – who are antagonistic to one another.

A political scientist has written that 'one of the liabilities of [women's] entry into public life remains the threat of character assassination by whisper and innuendo that is damaging to the honour of the women concerned. Women leaders conform publicly to the tradition of purdah, albeit symbolically and nationally, by covering their heads with their saris. Some degree of accommodation to the customs and values prescribed by religious-cultural traditions is necessary, for the national constituency remains conservative and imbued with patriarchal values.'

In a country where literacy rates are low for both men and women – but significantly lower for women – the government is trying to develop its educational resources. Of children six to ten years old, only about half are in school. The government in 1991 made universal primary education mandatory, but warned that it could not soon fully implement the law. Pilot programmes have been started, and in 1993 the government created a Division of Primary Education, separate from the Ministry of Education, to report directly to the Prime Minister's office. The education of girls will be a particular concern.

Bangladesh is one of the nations proving that efforts to limit population growth can work even in the poorest countries (life expectancy for both sexes is about 55). Average family size has fallen from seven children in 1970 to under five. The government is attempting to work with NGOs (non-governmental organizations) to achieve educational and other reforms.

Bangladesh has been said to have a 'nascent' women's movement, built on a variety of women's organizations: 'It is on issues concerning violence and oppression . . . that women's groups have responded with the most vigour.' In Bangladesh, women are still flogged, stoned, burned and disfigured by acid for giving 'moral offence'. A Cruelty to Women law has been on the books since 1983, but enforcement is weak, especially in rural areas where most people live.

As in other Muslim countries, an Islamic fundamentalist party is active in Bangladesh, and seeks to confine women to traditional ways of life. Hundreds of men came into the streets of Dhaka in the summer of 1994 to advocate death for a feminist author who outspokenly advocates female liberation, including sexual liberation, akin to that enjoyed by many women in the West.

DOMINICA

Dominica is one of the least developed of the Caribbean islands, with a small population of about 90,000. Approximately 80 percent of its people are Roman Catholics. Life expectancy is 80 years for women, 74 for men. The literacy rate for both sexes is equal at about 94 percent.

Dominica's economy has traditionally been heavily dependent upon its banana crop, which is sent to Great Britain. A land reform programme was put into effect after independence in 1978 and received wide support: large estates were acquired by the government, divided, and tenure granted to former workers. In 1989 there were about 13,000 female workers in a total island labour force of some 30,000. General unemployment was high in 1991 – approximately 15 percent. Less than 10 percent of the work force is unionized.

Dominica's prime minister was the first woman in the Caribbean to hold such office, and she has been active in regional institutions. Under her leadership, 'Dominica has become favoured as a recipient of international aid.' UN figures for 1987 showed women as nearly 13 percent of the country's parliament (House of Assembly), which has 30 members. As mentioned in chapter eight of this book, women have in some recent years held more than 20 percent of ministerial-level government positions. In the civil service, salaries are attached to a position and gender is irrelevant. However, there are no laws requiring equal pay for equal work in the private sector.

Problems for women in Dominica have included inheritance law (in 1993, a woman could not inherit property to sell if her husband died without a will, although she could live on the property) and sexual harassment, which is unregulated by law. The Welfare Department assists battered women, but in 1993 there was no long-term residence shelter available for them. Women's groups in Dominica have called for more programmes for pregnant teens and teenage mothers. (In 1992 the age of consent for sexual relations was raised from 14 to 16.) Women's rights groups have also sought legislation to govern domestic violence and sexual harassment.

FRANCE

Simone de Beauvoir, well-known writer and philosopher, stated that work is a *first* condition of independence; she also declared that 'la liberté de la femme commence au ventre' (women's freedom starts in the belly).

Women are doing quite well on these scores today in France: approximately 44 percent of French women work, and abortion was legalized by the French National Assembly in December of 1974. Access to abortion has become greater and greater, with state funding available in 1982. Contraceptives became widely and freely available in France in the late sixties.

Jane Jenson and Mariette Sineau have written of this country of 56 million people: 'Since the late nineteenth century France has had one of the highest rates of female labour-force participation and until recently one of the smallest gaps between women's and men's wages [around 30 to 35 percent in 1991]. It is, however, a country where the vision of wives as totally subordinate to husbands was not modified in the Napoleonic Code [which treated wives as, essentially, minors] until the middle of the twentieth century and where everyday language celebrates the difference between women and men.'

Attitudes dictating the role of women as culture-bearers, as highly significant presences within the home, go back into the nineteenth century, and made it prestigious for women not to work. The *femme au foyer* has been seen as a teacher of civilized values and an arranger of important functions in a culture that values the domestic circle and a high quality of daily living.

An ironic effect of the granting of the suffrage to French women in 1944 was their emergence as conservative voters. Only in the 1980s did French women appear in a new role, as more liberal voters than men, and as equally frequent casters of ballots. A study found that 'the factor most able to produce such a change [was] active participation in the labour force. Women in paid employment were much more likely than other women to participate in elections and vote for the Left, especially the Socialists.'

However, women remain few in elected office, especially at high levels. While approximately 17 percent of town councillors are women, in 1993 only 16 of 320 senators were women, and only 35 of 573 deputies of the lower house of the national legislature. According to Jenson and Sineau, French political parties 'continue to be clubbish and oligarchic institutions that are closed to women.' The Socialist Party has had statutes stipulating women's quotas for governing bodies inside the party, and for some candidacies (not the national legislature), but the quota system 'has not been respected inside the party organization, nor has much effort been made to elect women to the National Assembly.' Jenson and Sineau also maintain that 'the largest and most visible wings of the contemporary women's movement in France have never focused on the feminization of elected institutions.' A study showed that 'male politicians have an image of women politicians as constituting a tiny minority. Teased about being different, women politicians are reduced to their sex and considered inferior because of it.'

In 1993, a new development was a public campaign (stimulated by the publication of a book, *To Power, Women Citizens!*) for 'democratic parity' – an equal number of men and women in France's lower house. Also, the then-head of the Socialist Party, Michel Rocard, endorsed an 'equal numbers' party list for elections to the European Parliament.

ICELAND

Many of the things that women need to live decently and to develop are provided by Iceland's extensive social welfare system: 'There is a comprehensive system of social security, including old-age pensions, family allowances, maternity grants, widows pensions ... Pensions and health insurance now apply to the whole population. Accident insurance applies to all wage and salary earners and self-employed persons.'[1] Icelandic law even mandates adequate public day-care 'as part of the extensive "law of the child" passed by the Althing [parliament] in 1992.'[2] Prior to the 1992 law, one town (Akureyri) influenced by women's activism wrote into its budget that all single parents not able to get their children into the town's day-care centres were to receive money instead, 'for three, six, or nine months.'

Iceland is a small country of approximately 260,000 people, some 100,000 of whom live in the capital city of Reykjavik. An extraordinary event in Iceland's history was the 24 October 1975 Women's Strike – in which 90–95 percent of all Icelandic women refused to work for a day in order to demonstrate the force of women's labour and to protest against inequalities. In Reykjavik, according to police statistics, 25,000 women attended a rally. The success of the effort has been attributed to 'effective and comprehensive organization', involving almost all of Iceland's women's organizations, and an executive committee where all of the country's political parties and Iceland's largest labour unions were represented.

Social changes had occurred in Iceland in years prior to the Women's Strike. In 1964, only 28 percent of married women over the age of 16 held full- or part-time jobs. The numbers went up until by 1980 they were as high as 65 percent in the capital city. Women's educational level also rose: in 1970 only 15 percent of those graduating from the University of Iceland were women; by 1980 women were 41 percent. In 1970 the feminist revival which had begun to affect the United States and Europe came to Iceland in the form of the Redstocking movement – initiated by women who had few ties to older women's organizations in the country.

The Redstocking women had a varied agenda: they wanted free abortions, more money for day-care centres, equal pay and more power for women in political parties and labour unions. They were able to have some influence because of a leftist government (1971–74) which sympathized with their concerns. Also, although there were only three women in Iceland's parliament at the time, one of the three women (Svava Jakobsdóttir) became their spokeswoman. They thus complied with Gloria Steinem's injunction to 'surround the goal' by having activists both inside and outside of government.

The number of women in the Althing was to be tiny for many years. Between 1971 and 1983, for example, only three women were members, despite the fact that women's suffrage dated back to 1915. However, Iceland uses a proportional system of voting, and the introduction of women's lists in the early 1980s began to produce gains, first at the municipal level and then in parliament. In 1987 UN figures showed women to be one-fifth of the Althing's 60 members. Women's List is currently an active feminist political party. In the early 1990s not only was a woman president of Iceland, but women were also Chief Justice of the Supreme Court and Speaker of the Althing (the latter more of a ceremonial post than in most other nations).

Icelandic women do not have 'abortion on demand', but a law (of 1975) permitting doctors to decide on the sufficiency of grounds for abortions is very liberally construed.

Issues now for Women's List in Iceland include equal pay for equal work – overall there is a difference of 40 percent in earnings for women and men – and domestic violence and rape. Complaints have been that police and the courts are not sensitive to the latter issues. One improvement reported in 1993 was that the Reykjavik City Hospital emergency ward 'now has an all-female staff to care for rape victims.'[3]

IRELAND

Ireland – traditionally one of Europe's most conservative countries for women – is still a country of challenge. Irish women laboured hard, even went to prison, to get the vote in 1922. But they must still go abroad (usually to Britain) to get an abortion, and live in a culture where divorce remains constitutionally forbidden. Major battles were waged in this 95 percent Catholic country to make contraceptives widely available in the 1980s.

During her campaign for the presidency of Ireland, Mary Robinson made a remark which was supposed to have been, but turned out not to be, politically suicidal. She said: 'The whole patriarchal male-dominated presence of the [Catholic] church is probably the worst aspect of all the establishment forces that have sought to do down women over the years.' Ireland and Catholicism have been virtual synonyms; however, new forces are today on the scene. Ireland's participation in the European Economic Community creates legal obligations for the country, and these ties have affected the issues of abortion and homosexual rights in Ireland. The European Court of Human Rights ruled in 1988, for example, that Ireland had to decriminalize homosexuality.

In 1992 Ireland's voters declared in a national referendum that women have a right to abortion *information* – a position opposed by the Catholic Church. The voters, also, voted down a right to abortion on narrow grounds – an outcome welcomed by some feminists because the grounds were so limited. These women feel that other legal routes to wider abortion rights are to be pursued.

Ireland is a small country with a population of under four million people; traditionally agricultural, it is now nearly 60 percent urban. The majority of Ireland's women (some two-thirds or more) play traditional roles as wives and/or mothers and do not have wage-paying jobs; Ireland has fewer women in the labour force than any other European Community country. Complicating the situation for women who would like to work are an absence of social services and a very high overall unemployment rate (22 percent in 1993).

When they do hold jobs, a human rights report found that women 'are discriminated against in the areas of equal pay and promotion to senior positions in both the public and private sectors.' In 1993 the average hourly wage for women was 60 percent of what men received. In the Irish Civil Service, well over 90 percent of the senior-level jobs are held by men.

In 1990 the government established the Second Commission on the Status of Women to 'promote greater equality for women in all facets of Irish life', including training and education, employment opportunities, and legal rights. At the time the Commission was established, women did not have automatic joint ownership of the family home. There is a quasi-official Council for the Status of Women, representing over one hundred national women's organizations, that works on women's issues.

As might be expected, there are not large numbers of women in high elected national office in Ireland. However, in addition to having its first woman president, the country in October of 1993 saw the first woman elected leader of a national political party – Mary Harney of the Progressive Democrats. In the spring of 1993, about 20 of 166 members of the Dáil (legislative lower house) were women.

LITHUANIA

The major problem for women in Lithuania in recent years has been the economic struggle to survive. In 1992 '76 percent of families were officially reported to be living in poverty.'[1] The transition to a free-market economy has been difficult.

Lithuania is a country of approximately four million people, with substantial ethnic minorities of Russians, Poles and others. Most ethnic Lithuanians are Roman Catholics by belief or by family background. Under the new 1992 constitution, citizens are granted the right to 'old-age and disability pensions, as well as to social assistance in the event of unemployment, sickness, widowhood.'[2] A comprehensive state-funded health care system was introduced when Lithuania was still under Soviet domination; since independence, private medical practice has been legalized. Life expectancy for women was 76 in 1993 (it was nearly 10 years less for men). Women enjoy maternity and day-care benefits.

Lithuania's work force is employed in a number of different areas, including industrial production (food processing, light industry, machine building) and agriculture. Of the total 1989 labour force of just under two million, 941,000 workers were women. Unemployment has recently been low by most standards, but underemployment is a serious problem. An interesting footnote to Lithuania's labour situation is a shortage of trained lawyers – of either sex.

According to the US State Department, men and women generally 'receive the same pay for comparable work, but women are largely underrepresented in some professions and in the managerial sector as a whole.' They are also underrepresented in government 'for cultural and historical reasons': in 1993 only 10 members of the 141-member parliament (Seimas) were women, and there were no female ministers in the cabinet. One political party – the Lithuanian Green Party – was chaired by a woman, Irena Ignataviciene. Lithuania has two Chernobyl-type reactors, worrisome to some, and the issue of environmental pollution was on the agenda by the late 1980s.

A growing number of organizations which promote women's rights are active in Lithuania, but 'public awareness of women's issues is still at a rudimentary stage.' One problem for women is spouse abuse associated with alcoholism.

NETHERLANDS ANTILLES

The Netherlands Antilles has been called – to the annoyance of some – a 'rich developing country'. Despite hard times since the 1980s, the Holland-affiliated, five-island nation has reached a level of income well above that of other Caribbean countries. For example, the *Europa World Year Book* shows Netherlands Antilles as having a $7,395 per capita share of GNP in 1988, while Dominica, by way of comparison, is shown at $2,520 per capita in 1992 when GNP is divided by population. A well-developed union movement in Netherlands Antilles has helped keep wages high. Economic conditions vary substantially from island to island.

The country has a population of approximately 200,000. In 1983 the labour force of about 90,000 was 65 percent public sector employees. By 1988 the numbers had shifted – to about 58,000 employed and very substantial unemployment. In earlier years more money from oil refining and shipping had produced wealth to support government services. The oil refined in Netherlands Antilles is imported; the country lacks natural resources and does not even have much arable land. Food is imported also.

An educational system similar to that in Holland has produced a high adult literacy rate in the country, about 95 percent for both sexes. The political and religious circumstances of each of the five islands vary. Political parties are indigenous to each island, and three of the islands are mostly Roman Catholic, while two are mostly Protestant. Life expectancy in 1993 was about comparable to that in the US: 78 years for women (four or five less for men).

Work outside the home is seen as 'normal' and 'nothing new' for women in the country. Women work in the public sector, in the usual 'women's professions' (such as teaching and nursing) and as, less frequently, businesswomen, attorneys, or other professionals. The president of one business association is currently a woman. Women have led major parties, and two are currently government ministers. A handful of women are in parliament; one chairs the legislative body. Because women *do* work outside the home, one of their greatest needs is the sharing of housework and childrearing duties.

Issues of violence against women are also on the country's feminist agenda. There are no laws against marital rape, and there is no shelter for battered women on any of the five islands. Women who need to escape from abusive men sometimes go to Holland.

Interestingly, although abortion is not legal in Netherlands Antilles, it is 'not an issue'. Women 'know where to go', according to a women's activist.[1]

NICARAGUA

As has been typical for women in Central and South America, Nicaraguan women, prior to the revolution of 1979, were part of a gender division which 'ties women to their home and family in a subservient position, while men ... occupy positions of leadership in all spheres, particularly the public political one'. This division has been traditionally discussed in relation to the concepts of *marianismo* and *machismo* – the first requiring women to be humble and virtuous (literally 'like the Virgin Mary') and the latter expressing male self-assertion, autonomy and dominance.

Under a series of Somoza-family dictators, social conditions in Nicaragua were so repressive and impoverishing that 'mass poverty caused family disintegration. Men without work ... frequently abandoned their families, going off to search for jobs. Women found themselves alone, with responsibility for home and children.' In 1963, for example, census figures showed 25 percent of the households in Managua, the capital, to be headed by women. Because they had no choice, 'larger numbers of women in Nicaragua came to participate in the labour force than in other Latin American countries where repression was less acute.' Statistics from the OAS (Organization of American States) in 1979 'showed Nicaragua leading the rest of Central America in the percentage of females in the total work force.'

In the 1960s, Nicaragua began to slowly move towards revolution. One researcher has compared the involvement of women in guerrilla movements in five countries. She found that 'women took part in every phase of the Revolution to overthrow Somoza and made up 30 percent of the FSLN guerrilla membership at the time of the final offensive' in 1979. Women took part in strikes and demonstrations, hid combatants and weaponry in 'safe houses', and, towards the end, led major military offensives. The new revolutionary government 'supported the women's movement and recognized the need to address and respond to women's issues.' AMNLAE, a new women's organization aligned with the government, was founded, and was named for the first woman (Luisa Amanda Espinoza) who died fighting Somoza's National Guard.

Under the new government, 'alimony and child support became newly legislated rights. Common-law marriages, the most typical kind, and "illegitimate" children, the majority of all children, were now recognized.' Laws such as the 'Law of Nurturing' assigned equal responsibility for childrearing to men and women both. However, abortion rights were not one of the rights given to women – the subject is too sensitive in Catholic Nicaragua, even though unsafe abortions have been the main cause of maternal deaths.

Today, the situation for women in Nicaragua is shaped by the extreme poverty caused by a decade of US-funded war. The well documented gains in literacy and public health conditions achieved by the Sandinista government have been eroded. Diseases like cholera are on the increase, infant mortality has been increasing, and diarrhea has become the most common cause of death among Nicaraguan children. Government spending on health and other social services has been cut, partly at the behest of international lenders, and non-governmental organizations are struggling to maintain health and family planning services with private contributions. Unemployment and underemployment are commonly assessed to run as high as 50 to 70 percent. Many of Nicaragua's approximately four million people are seriously malnourished.

In 1987 about 13 percent of parliamentary seats in the national legislature were held by women. According to the US State Department, in 1993 women 'occupied some senior positions in government, the trade union movement, and social organizations, but were underrepresented in management positions in the private sector and formed the majority of workers in the traditionally low-paid educational, textile and health service sectors.'[1]

In the past few years women's groups independent of AMNLAE have strengthened in Nicaragua. An organizer for La Malinche, one such group, stated: 'We won't set up clinics . . . We target patriarchy more than the government. Above all we don't ask anyone's permission to be feminists.'[2] In 1992 some groups joined together to form the National Feminist Committee (CNF).

NORWAY

Norway – a country of 4.3 million people with egalitarian traditions – impresses an observer on many fronts. Not only does it have a parliament (the Storting) which is approximately one third women (with women also one third of municipal councils and equally or even more frequent on county councils), but its highly developed social welfare benefits include national health insurance (abortions are paid for as part of health services); extensive maternity leave with full pay; legally mandated worker vacations of 25 or 31 days per year (the latter for workers over 60); and a legal work week of 37.5 hours. Norway's women began coming into the labour force in large numbers in the

1970s; currently, about 70 percent of women work.

Historically, Norway has had many 'firsts' for women. It was, for example, the first country in the world to allow daughters to inherit legally with sons, in 1854. For a brief time (three years) after World War II, the work of women in the house was counted as part of the country's Gross National Product, until Norway was forced to give up the practice in order to comply with international labour standards. Women obtained the national vote in 1913, second in Europe only to Finland (1906).

Some women's organizations in Norway date back into the nineteenth or early twentieth century; political parties and trade unions have had women's branches (Norway is heavily unionized, with membership about 60 percent of the work force). In recent years three major parties have been simultaneously headed by women.

As noted in chapter eight of this book, several years of effort were needed in order to raise the number of women in elected office in Norway to present levels. Agitation for more women on party candidate lists began at the municipal level in 1967. Write-in provisions of electoral laws allowed the scratch-out of men's names and the writing-in of women's names. These electoral provisions were changed at some points by political parties when women appeared to be gaining too many seats. Year by year, however, inroads were made.

One researcher found that 'the most effective, overarching strategy developed by Norwegian women activists' to promote change was 'the building of a strong coalition'[1] between older and newer women's organizations: 'After the mid–1970s, the establishment women and the new feminists created a tightly knit network of committees which worked on getting party nominations of female candidates and their placement in top positions on election ballots. Moreover, a concerted effort was made to develop policies catering to women's interests and to gain acceptance of such policies by political parties.'[2]

Norway has an Equal Status Act (ESA) passed in 1978 to promote 'equal pay for work of equal value'. According to one researcher, 'the bill has not resolved the ominous wage differences between the sexes, despite the longevity of this important issue';[3] typically, women work in lower-paid and substantially sex-segregated fields. Norwegian women have not been able to influence the business world as they have the political, nor have union groups always been on their side.

In 1981 the ESA was amended by parliament in an important way: to provide that government-appointed public committees, boards, and councils have a 40 percent women representation.

Since women hold many jobs in the public sector in Norway (70 percent of state employees are women), cuts in public services caused by difficult economic times can affect women's jobs disproportionately, and also disrupt the 'safety net' which strengthens their lives.

Norway is a country where crime against women is not widespread; marital rape is recognized in the law; access to abortion in the first twelve weeks of pregnancy has been a 'civil right' since 1978; and a government funded network of shelters for battered women is well developed. The country needs more child-care and kindergarten services.

PAKISTAN

The situation for many women (and children) in Pakistan today is so deleterious to their welfare as to be almost unbelievable to a late twentieth-century observer.

Primary education is not (de facto) compulsory in this country of 130 million people, despite a 1962 law that was to have begun the process of mandatory primary education. Child labour is widespread, with 'unofficial estimates' that 'one-third of Pakistan's total labor force of thirty-three million is made up of workers under age 18.' The Employment of Children Act of 1991 set seven hours as the maximum workday for children under fourteen, in a country where the law provides for a maximum workweek of 54 hours. A study found that approximately a million children are engaged in the cottage industry of weaving carpets, which are a Pakistani export; these children had either never been to school or had dropped out. In the absence of mandatory primary education, Pakistan's high illiteracy rate of 75–85 percent is not surprising.

UNICEF (the United Nations Children's Fund) has found that Pakistan has one of the highest reported ratios of males to females in the world. Boys are preferred, and receive family resources, including calories. Women are discriminated against in every area of life – despite their agricultural labour alongside men's in a country that is three quarters rural-and they do not have equal legal rights. In 1992 the country's Supreme Court invalidated the requirement that a husband give written notice of a divorce to a local council. A husband can simply say (or deny) that he has divorced his wife. In one situation in 1993, a lower court sentenced an 'adulteress' to be stoned to death, and her second husband flogged one hundred lashes, when her first husband denied he had divorced her. Fortunately the couple were able to produce evidence that they believed themselves married. They were acquitted on appeal.

During the martial law regime of General Mohammed Zia ul-Haq, laws called the Hudood ordinances were passed regarding adultery, fornication, rape and prostitution. Under the ordinances, four witnesses must testify that a woman has been raped – otherwise, her behaviour may be considered adultery or fornication, punishable by stoning to death or flogging. A woman's testimony in court carries half the legal weight of a man's. The Hudood ordinances have not been seriously challenged by any government since they were created.

In 1991 a Shariat bill was passed which called for 'bringing all aspects of government and society in Pakistan into conformity with the tenets of Islam.' On 4 December 1992 the *Toronto Star* reported that all women on state-run television had been ordered to wear Muslim head scarves; radio stations had been ordered to drop hundreds of songs regarded as socially or religiously inappropriate; and Pakistan's penal code had been altered to make execution mandatory for anyone who 'directly or indirectly defiles the sacred name of the Holy Prophet'.

According to the *Star*, 'militant mullahs have always been a voice in the corridors of power in Islamabad.' One consequence: in 1985 religious minorities lost the right to vote in the same manner as Sunni Muslims; minorities vote from separate rolls for a limited number of 'reserved seats' in parliament.

Women, too, have in the past had 'reserved seats'. These were dropped in 1990, and two parties have pledged to restore them. However, their tokenism is a reason they can be supported. In the spring of 1991 the 217-member National Assembly contained only two women, Benazir Bhutto and Nusrat Bhutto. However, in 1975 women held 4 percent of the seats, and in 1987, 9 percent. Women received the vote in 1947, when India and Pakistan became independent from Britain.

There are professional women, working particularly in the fields of teaching, medical services and the law, in Pakistan. In Karachi, there are a substantial number of women judges in the civil courts. Women's organizations exist throughout the country, but are concentrated in urban centres.

Pakistan's population is rising at a rapid rate, and could reach 300 million by the year 2020 without better family planning services. These are opposed by Islamic fundamentalist scholars and village clergy. Pakistan appears on a list of UN countries that spent more for the military than for health and education combined in both 1960 and 1986. Life expectancy is in the mid-fifties.

Domestic violence in the country is considered a private matter; marital rape is not a crime under Pakistani law, and 'rape of another man's wife is a common method of seeking revenge in rural and tribal areas.' An organization called WAR (War Against Rape) has taken on the issue, and found in studying 60 rape cases in Lahore that members of police forces were substantially implicated. Women in police custody in Pakistan have faced sexual and physical abuse. In January of 1994 international press photographs showed Prime Minister Bhutto opening Pakistan's first police station staffed exclusively by women.

THE PHILIPPINES

The Philippines, a basically agricultural country of 61 million, has had educated women and active women's organizations since the first decades of the twentieth century. It was because of both that a remarkably determined fight for the suffrage could end in success in 1937. When the all male legislature of the time established that the right to vote would be given to women only if – in a national plebiscite – no fewer than 300,000 women voted in its favour, women organized so well throughout the country that they surpassed their goal by almost 150,000 votes.

Women were also active at this time in social movements directed against US colonial rule, as a few had been active in earlier movements against Spanish colonialism. One researcher has summed up: 'From the beginning of the [twentieth] century to the outbreak of World War II . . . women in the Philippines . . . were launched into a new world altogether after centuries of enforced domesticity, illiteracy and cruel repression under Spanish rule.'

After the World War II Japanese occupation, the Philippines became independent in 1946. Between 1946 and 1972, when Ferdinand Marcos declared martial law, a tiny number of women were elected to the national legislature (18), to be governors (6), or to be city mayors (2). Many more held lesser civic posts.

By the 1970s some women had become active in radical groups responding to the country's prevalent poverty: the social structure of the Philippines remained, as it had since the Spaniards, rooted in a small, wealthy, landowning class. Women became guerrilla fighters in the New People's Army, or active with MAKIBA (Free Movement of New Women), which held mass actions, established cottage industries and helped set up day-care centres. Activist nuns, influenced by liberation theology, worked to assist political prisoners and the urban poor. GABRIELA, another group, protested the US military bases that remained on Philippine soil, and the extensive prostitution (involving many thousands of women) that was associated with them. The corruption of the Marcos regime extended to the fact that his government promoted 'sex tourism' to bring money into the economy: 'The Ministry of Tourism regularly conducted sex tours for male visitors . . . Never before had Filipinas been so degraded.'

After the assassination of Benigno Aquino, Jr. in 1983 'women from all classes and persuasions worked side by side in challenging the [Marcos] dictatorship.' Large women's organizations involved were GABRIELA and KABAPA (New Filipino Women's Association), the latter a force among rural women. Many other groups came into the streets during the final days of People's Power. With the election of Corazon Aquino, women had one of their own at the top.

The Philippines today remains poor, with an undeveloped safety net, and with opposition from the Catholic Church to birth control measures. In February of 1993, for example, Cardinal Sin – an important ally of People's Power – 'organized a rally in Manila, attended by 300,000 Catholics, to denounce the birth control policies of the Ramos administration, following the Secretary of Health's public promotion of prophylactics to limit the spread of AIDS.'[1] In 1993, also, poor women were 'extensively victimized by international sex trafficking syndicates, which recruited them to work abroad.'[2] Domestic violence and rape are serious problems, and marital rape is not a crime under the law.

Women hold a small number of seats in the national legislature. In 1993, 19 women served in the House (out of 202 members); three women (of 23) were senators. As mentioned elsewhere, three women were appointed by Corazon Aquino to the Supreme Court. Many women work in public administration, with the numbers in high-level positions well above what is typical around the world. The Philippine Military Academy began admitting females in 1993.

Illiteracy in the Philippines is about 10 percent for both sexes. Women who are 'economically active' are 46 percent of all women.

POLAND

Feminist efforts in Poland go well back into the nineteenth century, and focused then on the right to an education. In 1918 came the vote and the right to be elected. In the 1920s and 1930s women were a small fraction (between two and five percent) of the two houses of the national legislature.

Under the Communist regime which came to power after World War II, an ideological emphasis on sexual equality brought more women into parliament, until in the mid–1980s women were about 23 percent of the Sejm (lower house). They were not, however, highly represented in the very important Communist Party major posts. Nor were they many in top positions in Solidarity when (and while) the trade union began challenging the Communist Party for control of Poland – even though women are believed to have made up half of the rank-and-file of Solidarity, just as they made up about one half of the Polish labour force by the mid–1980s.

During its period of rule, the Communist Party urged women to enter the work force and help Poland industrialize. The country ceased being largely agricultural as people migrated to cities. Educational opportunities were expanded and 'women were provided with free health care, job and wage protection during pregnancy, and 16 weeks of maternity leave with salary . . . In 1971, a new law went even further by allowing a woman with a child four years old or younger a three-year unpaid leave.'

In 1980, when Solidarity was formed and began to negotiate with the Communist regime, a 'three-year paid maternity leave was the only provision directly concerning women. In addition, Solidarity pushed for the expansion of kindergarten and nursery facilities for working mothers . . . In essence, they continued the view expressed by the Communists that women are equal, but some are weaker and have a different role to perform. What the shipyard workers wanted to see was women in their traditional role as wives and mothers. . . '

When Solidarity was forced underground in December of 1981, active 'women who avoided being interned were left with full responsibility for their families and their imprisoned partners.' The government could not, however, govern Poland without the participation of the forces that Solidarity represented – disaffection was too great. Martial law was ended in July of 1983. Strikes in 1988 helped bring about major negotiations in early 1989 for a change of regime ('not even one woman was a chief negotiator').

Political and economic restructuring have brought this country of 38 million people new institutions and freedoms. However, 'women and the elderly (who are predominantly women) have become increasingly vulnerable ... Indeed, women are the majority of the new unemployed and have already lost their right to long-term parental leave.' Their numbers in parliament have fallen (in 1991 they constituted about 9 percent of the Sejm and 6 percent of the upper house); in 1990 they took about 10 percent of the seats in local councils. Women have lost the liberal abortion rights put into effect in 1956, under which abortion was more or less fully available and free.

After three years of controversy, beginning in 1989, President Lech Walesa (in February of 1992) signed an anti-abortion law 'with strict limits and sentences of up to two years in prison for doctors who violate the rules.'[1] An unintended consequence of the controversy was the formation of new women's organizations, and the mobilization of older ones, around the abortion issue. But these groups were not the equals in strength of the Catholic Church, conservative forces and President Walesa himself.

Today about 43 percent of Poland's women are in the work force. Ironically, even though 'women's educational attainment has risen faster than men's during the last 40 years,' and women 'now constitute a majority in general secondary schools and universities,'[2] men 'can find jobs more easily': 'The available jobs are incompatible with the skills possessed by women, for the majority ... are for manual labourers. Unemployed women have more education than unemployed men, and this difference is especially pronounced among young people.'[3]

SRI LANKA

Sri Lanka, an island nation south of India, is today the home of approximately 18 million people, about two thirds of them under 30 years of age. Most – 80 percent – live in rural areas, and a large proportion of the population (46 percent) works in agriculture, including tea culture, a major export crop.

Rural workers – including women – face low wages and sometimes poor living conditions, but Sri Lanka has had social welfare policies that have produced very creditable records of health and literacy. Life expectancy for women in 1993 was 74 years (it was five years less for men); the literacy rate in 1990 was 84 percent for women (and higher for men: 93 percent). The 1 March 1994 issue of the *International Herald Tribune* reported that Sri Lanka 'has the most educated workers in South Asia.' Not unrelatedly, it also reported that the country was having 'the most sustained economic growth in South Asia'.

The lives of women in Sri Lanka are affected by the civil war (in which women have taken part as fighters) between the government and Tamil rebels. According to the US State Department, between 1991 and 1993 one of the prisoners held by the 'Tamil Tigers' was Thiagarajah Selvanithy, a poet and women's activist. Also affecting women's lives are the particular cultures of the ethnic or religious groups to which they belong. Sri Lanka is approximately 69 percent Buddhist, 15 percent Hindu, and 8 percent (each) Muslim and Christian. While 'Sri Lankan women have equal rights under national civil and criminal law,' matters related to 'marriage, divorce, child custody, and inheritance', for example, 'are subject at the local level to the customary law of each particular ethnic or religious group,' including, for Muslims, Islamic law.

While there are 'no de jure impediments to women's participation in politics or government . . . the social mores of some communities have the effect of limiting women's participation in activities outside the home.' While there are women at senior levels of government service, only 11 (out of 225) members of parliament were women in 1993. Women have been able to vote since 1931.

Like nearly all societies today, Sri Lanka has many women professionals, and more coming up. In the early 1980s nearly one half of university students in medical, dental and veterinary courses were women. Articles on women's problems have appeared in newspapers in all three major languages – Sinhala, Tamil and English – since about 1975. In the booming garment industry, where 200,000 work, the vast majority are young women.

Domestic violence and sexual assault are reported to be 'common' in Sri Lanka, but are often not reported for cultural and social reasons. Women's organizations have taken up these issues, including 'violence directed against female domestic servants', but 'the Government has yet to deal effectively with these issues', according to a 1993 US State Department report.

TURKEY

Turkey is a surprising and paradoxical country where women are concerned. On the one hand, it has a strong tradition of professional working women – doctors, attorneys, and others – who derive from urban, well-off families. A far greater number of women in Turkey come from rural villages (although they may be urban migrants), may be illiterate (as are half of Turkish women), may be poor, and sometimes face Turkey's widespread problem of spouse abuse.

Turkey's population size (57 million) is about the same as that of France, but Turkey's women received the vote in 1934, ten years sooner than French women. If this is unexpected, so is the fact that Turkey's most progressive women's period, it could be argued, came in the 1920s and 1930s, and was greatly attributable to a man: Mustafa Kemal Atatürk. Atatürk, who led Turkey's three-year (1919–1922) war for independence, believed that modern democracy depends on the participation of both sexes; he had a personal interest in women's rights.

When Turkey was established as a republic in 1923, its constitution defined the state as secular, with legal codes derived from

Europe, and the state granted women full rights of citizenship. This historical period is known as the period of 'state feminism'. In some of the years following, Turkey had more women in parliament than it has had since.

Turkey today has many women judges in one part of its court system, and it has large numbers of women working in government (women are 29 percent of civil servants – and receive equal pay and pensions with men). There are women in the army who have risen to colonel. But there are very few women in elected office: in 1991 eight of 450 members of parliament were women, and only one of Turkey's current appointed governors, out of 74, is a woman. Turkey had only ten women mayors between 1950 and 1980. Few women are elected to municipal councils. According to researchers, 'political life continues to be dominated by parties only sometimes interested in or friendly towards women.'

Turkey is 98 percent Muslim. Today 'Islamic revivalists have started a campaign to control women's sexuality and life opportunities [which] stresses their role as wives and mothers.' The conflict between Turkey's twentieth century tradition of secular government and its Islamic religionists – a conflict whose outcome is critical to the future of women – is played out in many arenas, including that of dress codes in the universities. Both 'law and custom require women and men who work in the public sector or attend public universities to dress secularly.' Followers of Islam have held demonstrations and sit-ins promoting the wearing of the Islamic head scarf in the universities. The issue reached the courts. Since 1982 'religious culture' must be taught in primary and secondary schools.

Turkey has abortion rights for women to the tenth week of pregnancy without the need to prove a medical justification; however, married women must obtain notarized consent from their husbands. Unlike in most countries, 'the right to abortion was not granted as a result of a continual struggle by women's associations.' It was, instead, granted by an outgoing military government(!) in 1983. Military governments took over Turkey in 1960–61, 1971–73 and 1980–83.

Turkey's birthrate continues to be high, its family planning services not very successful, its 'safety net' undeveloped and its child-care centres and kindergartens few and expensive. Further educational development of its people is a concern: men are one quarter illiterate, and a 1992 law increasing mandatory education from five years to eight will be implemented gradually throughout the country. Traditional values in rural Turkey emphasize education for sons more than for daughters. Illiteracy prevents women from learning of their rights or shared problems. In major cities like Istanbul and Ankara, women university scholars research and seek to address the problems of Turkey's women, as do women's organizations. In May of 1989 the 'Second Women's Convention' drew 2,500 women to Istanbul to hear more than 70 papers on issues of concern.

UNITED KINGDOM OF GREAT BRITAIN AND NORTHERN IRELAND

British women received the vote, cautiously, in two stages: in 1918 for women over 30; in 1928 at the same (younger) age as men. As in France, the early years of women's voting showed females to be more conservative than males; in the 1980s, again as in France, the 'gender gap' reversed. According to one researcher, neither of Britain's two major parties – Labour or the Conservatives – paid much attention to women party members or voters *until* the 1980s. One factor in their change was the appearance in 1980 of a new party, the Social Democratic, which pledged to achieve greater sexual equality. The Social Democrats, Liberal Democrats and Labour all introduced some party quotas for women in the 1980s.

Britain's long tradition of democracy has produced 'a highly traditional society with a centralized, secretive and bureaucratically dominated system'.[1] Several factors have made it hard for women to gain power in government: a powerful 'old boys' ('chaps') network, feeding its male members into apprenticeship pipelines; a lack of significant decision making at a regional level, as in the United States, which would make for more positions of power; and a system without a written constitution, to help reform through law. A factor now working in women's favour is Britain's membership in the European Economic Community, which obligates its member states to sexual equality in pay, employment, and social security provisions. The European Court of Justice, for example, directed Britain to improve its administration of the country's Equal Pay Act, on the books since 1970.

According to Joyce Gelb, 'most women-oriented legislation in Britain did not come about as a result of pressure from feminists, but rather from political parties and trade unions,'[2] the two major sources of power. 'In the Labour Party, for example, the traditional industrial unions have had nominating rights and, as such, a great deal of influence over the choice of parliamentary candidates. Many unions continue to support candidates that come from their ranks; these candidates typically are white men.'[3] Tony Blair, now leader of the Labour Party, has instituted changes in party-union relationships which have subsequently affected union powers. But at present only about 60 of 650 members in the House of Commons are women. Nor are women often found 'in ministerial office, in the senior ranks of higher civil service, or in the higher judiciary'.[4]

It has not helped the political power of women in Great Britain that its women's movement has been very highly fragmented. There have been many localized groups with a great many projects and with widely divergent views on the relationship of women to society and to men. Activity surrounding abortion rights has been 'perhaps the most sustained and widespread of all women's political participation in Britain'.[5] The country does not have 'abortion on demand', but it has a 1967 Abortion Law Reform Act which has been very liberally construed by medical professionals who must decide on a woman's right to an abortion. (This law does not apply to Northern Ireland.) Women have had to defend the 1967 act against efforts to make abortion more restricted: they have successfully done so, at times with the help of the trade unions.

Great Britain (England, Scotland and Wales) has a population that is about the same size as that of France or Turkey; about 45 percent of the country's women work.

Endnotes

Introduction

1) A few living women have served in these positions for less time, provisionally, or under circumstances that were atypical (for example, their country no longer exists as it was – Yugoslavia).

Chapter 1 – Biographies

1) *Wall Street Journal*, 7 May 1987

2) *New York Times*, 3 July 1993

3) *Lear's*, October 1993

4) *Guardian*, 7 May 1991

5) *Observer*, 16 June 1991

6) *New York Times*, 8 September 1982

Chapter 2 – Politics Sans Intent

1) Maritess D Vitug. 'Interview with Cory Aquino', *Filipinas*, March 1993, 60.

2) Jana Everett. 'Indira Gandhi and the Exercise of Power', in *Women as National Leaders*, ed. Michael A Genovese (Newbury Park, CA: SAGE Publications, 1993), 112.

3) 'During the 1960s and 1970s, when male deputies were removed from office by the military government, their wives were occasionally elected to fill their places, a Brazilian variant of the "widow's succession".' Jane S Jaquette. 'Female Participation in Latin America: Raising Feminist Issues', in *Women in the World, 1975–1985, The Women's Decade*, ed. Lynne B Iglitzin & Ruth Ross (Santa Barbara: ABC-CLIO, 1986), 248.

4) The latter route was used by Nancy Astor to become the first woman MP (in 1919). See Ruth Ross. 'Tradition and Women in

Great Britain', in *Women in the World: A Comparative Study*, ed. Lynne B Iglitzin & Ruth Ross (Santa Barbara: Clio Books, 1976), 168.

5) Linda Witt, Karen M Paget, and Glenna Matthews. *Running as a Woman: Gender and Power in American Politics* (New York: The Free Press, 1994), 31.

6) See, for example, Garry Wills. *Certain Trumpets: The Call of Leaders* (New York: Simon and Schuster, 1994): '[The leader] takes others toward the object of their joint quest.'

7) Everett in *Women as National Leaders*, 127.

8) See, for example, the stories of Madeleine Kunin and Ann Richards, two US governors, in Witt et al., *Running as a Woman*, 86.

9) Carol M Ostrom. 'Cleaning House in Government', *Seattle Times/Seattle Post-Intelligencer*, 2 August 1992, sec. A.

CHAPTER 3 – BACKGROUNDS

1) In July of 1994, the news media were reporting that India's parliament, hoping to prevent the widespread abortion of females, had passed a law to prevent doctors from telling would-be parents the sex of fetuses. Girls require a costly dowry at marriage. India has a long history of female infanticide.

2) Nancy Fix Anderson. 'Benazir Bhutto and Dynastic Politics: Her Father's Daughter, Her People's Sister', in *Women as National Leaders*, 54.

3) Anderson in *Women as National Leaders*, 45.

4) According to Olga S Opfell. *Women Prime Ministers and Presidents* (Jefferson, NC: McFarland & Co., 1993), 70.

5) Michael A Genovese. 'What Do We Know?', in *Women as National Leaders*, 214.

6) Torill Stokland, Mallica Vajrathon, Davidson Nicols, eds. *Creative Women in Changing Societies: A Quest for Alternatives* (Dobbs Ferry, NY: Transnational Publishers, 1982), 23.

7) Stokland et al. *Creative Women in Changing Societies*, 24.

8) Patricia Lee Sykes. 'Women as National Leaders: Patterns and Prospects', in *Women as National Leaders*, 220–24.

9) Ron Arias & Fred Hauptfuhrer. 'Here's to You, Mrs. Robinson', *People*, 26 November 1990, 57.

CHAPTER 4 – THROUGH A DIFFERENT LENS

1) Stephen Engelberg. 'Her Year of Living Dangerously', *The New York Times Magazine*, 12 September 1993.

2) Claudia Dreifus. 'Benazir Bhutto', *The New York Times Magazine*, 15 May 1994.

3) Michael A Genovese & Seth Thompson. 'Women as Chief Executives: Does Gender Matter?', in *Women as National Leaders*, 4.

4) For interesting tales concerning women politicians and their problems with dress, see Witt et al. *Running as a Woman*, 56–60.

CHAPTER 5 – LEADERSHIP STYLES

1) Michael A Genovese in *Women as National Leaders*, 24.

2) Lawrence Stone. Review of *A History of Women in the West* in *New Republic*, 2 May 1994, 34.

3) Jane Mansbridge in *Harvard Business Review*, 156.

4) Introduction Speech for International Hall of Fame. Copy provided by President Chamorro's staff.

5) Michael A Genovese in *Women as National Leaders*, 198.

6) Michael A Genovese in *Women as National Leaders*, 198.

7) Women are often said to 'personalize' politics. Former US President Ronald Reagan became famous for his use – or abuse – of 'personal examples' in public performances.

8) Lyn Kathlene. 'Studying the New Voice of Women in Politics', *The Chronicle of Higher Education*, 18 November 1992, B2.

9) Sykes in *Women as National Leaders*, 226.

10) Sykes in *Women as National Leaders*, 227.

11) Sykes in *Women as National Leaders*, 227.

12) Sykes in *Women as National Leaders*, 228.

CHAPTER 6 – THE TOUGHNESS REALM

1) Michael A Genovese. 'Margaret Thatcher and the Politics of Conviction Leadership', in *Women as National Leaders*, 193.

2) Witt et al. *Running as a Woman*, 2 & 228.

3) 'Violence is something we women abhor.' Corazon Aquino to Maritess D Vitug, *Filipinas*, March 1993, 59.

4) Dreifus. 'Benazir Bhutto'.

5) Dreifus. 'Benazir Bhutto'.

6) Witt et al. *Running as a Woman*, 227.

7) Witt et al. *Running as a Woman*, 30.

8) Witt et al. *Running as a Woman*, 30.

CHAPTER 7 – HEROES AND HELPERS

1) Social Democratic leader and chancellor of West Germany from 1969–74.

2) Chairman of the Social Democratic Party in Sweden and prime minister of Sweden (1969–76, 1982–6).

3) French national heroine, lived 1412–1431.

4) Leader of Yugoslavia from 1943–80.

5) President of Egypt from 1956–70.

6) Influential advocate of non-violence and Indian nationalist leader, assassinated in 1948.

7) US civil rights leader, assassinated in 1968.

8) Dissident, playwright and currently president of the Czech Republic.

9) French general and president of the Fifth French Republic (1958–69).

10) Prime minister of Great Britain from 1940–5 and 1951–5.

11) President of France since 1981.

12) In the West the tradition of arranged marriages is reflected in this passage from the great French writer Michel de Montaigne (from 'On Some Verses of Virgil'): 'Connections and means have, with reason, as much weight in [marriage] as graces and beauty, or more. We do not marry for ourselves, whatever we say; we marry just as much or more for our posterity, for our family. The practice and benefit of marriage concerns our race very far beyond us. Therefore I like this fashion of arranging it rather by a third hand than by our own, and by the sense of others rather than by our own.'

13) Dreifus. 'Benazir Bhutto'.

14) Dreifus. 'Benazir Bhutto'.

15) Stone. Review of *A History of Women in the West*.

16) Stone. Review of *A History of Women in the West*.

CHAPTER 8 – ONE HALF OF THE WORLD

1) *Los Angeles Times*, 29 June 1993.

2) *The World's Women 1970–1990, Trends and Statistics*, Social Statistics and Indicators, Series K, No. 8 (United Nations, New York, 1991).

3) One such group is the new international women's rights project (directed by Dorothy Thomas) of Human Rights Watch.

4) Most countries of the world use some form of proportional voting. New Zealand has recently converted to one. The US, Great Britain, Canada, and France (the last at the national parliamentary level only) are exceptions to the general picture.

5) Jill M Bystydzienski. 'Influence of Women's Culture on Public Politics in Norway', in *Women Transforming Politics*, ed. Jill M Bystydzienski (Bloomington and Indianapolis: Indiana University Press, 1992), 20–21.

6) Bystydzienski in *Women Transforming Politics*, 21.

7) Bystydzienski in *Women Transforming Politics*, 21.

8) Bystydzienski in *Women Transforming Politics*, 22.

CHAPTER 9 – GEOGRAPHY AND GENDER

Country Notes (in alphabetical order)

Material for country notes was derived from many sources, including *Country Reports on Human Rights Practices for 1993*, prepared by the US Department of State and published in February of 1994. Also consulted were data in *The Europa World Year Book*, Volume I, 1994, and Volume II, 1993. Other major sources of information are listed by country. A wide variety of newspaper and magazine articles are not specifically cited, but some references are given in the country histories themselves.

Bangladesh

The quotations cited are all from Najma Chowdhury. 'Bangladesh: Gender Issues and Politics in a Patriarchy', in *Women and Politics Worldwide*, eds. Barbara J Nelson and Najma Chowdhury (New Haven and London: Yale University Press, 1994), 100–1, 102, 105.

Dominica

The one quotation cited is from *The Europa World Year Book*, Volume I, 1994.

France

All quotations except that from Simone de Beauvoir are from Jane Jenson & Mariette Sineau. 'The Same or Different: An Unending Dilemma of French Women', *Women in Politics Worldwide*, 246, 248, 249.

Iceland

The quotations cited, except for 1–3, are from Audur Styrkársdóttir. 'From Social Movement to Political Party: The New Women's Movement in Iceland' in *The New Women's Movement*, ed. Drude Dahlerup (London: SAGE Publications, 1986), 142, 143, 147 & 155. Other quotations are as follows: 1. *Europa World Year Book*, Vol. I, 1994, 1416. 2. *Country Reports on Human Rights Practices*, 920. 3. *Country Reports on Human Rights Practices*, 920.

Ireland

Except for President Mary Robinson's famous quotation, which has been printed in a number of places, the quotations are from *Country Reports on Human Rights Practices*, 924.

Lithuania

Quotations 1 & 2 are from *Europa World Year Book*, Vol. II, 1993, 1806. Any other quotations are from *Country Reports on Human Rights Practices*, 959.

Netherlands Antilles

The quotation cited is from a telephone conversation with Jacqueline Martis, 29 September 1994.

Nicaragua

The quotations cited, except for 1 and 2, are from Barbara J Seitz. 'From Home to Street: Women and Revolution in Nicaragua', in *Women Transforming Politics*, ed. Jill M Bystydzienski (Bloomington & Indianapolis: Indiana University Press, 1992), 163, 166, 167, 168 and 172. Quotation 1 is from *Country Reports on Human Rights Practices*, 510. Quotation 2 is from *Report on the Americas*, XXVI, 4, February 1993, 13.

Norway

The first two quotations are from Jill M Bystydzienski. 'Influence of Women's Culture on Public Politics in Norway', in *Women Transforming Politics*, 12, 13. Quotation 3 is from Janneke van der Ros. 'The State and Women: A Troubled Relationship in Norway', in *Women and Politics Worldwide*, 535.

Pakistan

All quotations are from *Country Reports on Human Rights Practices*, 1381, 1382 & 1386.

The Philippines

All of the quotations except 1 & 2 are from Belinda A. Aquino. 'Philippine Feminism in Historical Perspective', in *Women and Politics Worldwide*, 596, 597, 600 & 601. Quotation 1 is from *Europa World Year Book*, Vol. II, 1993. Quotation 2 is from *Country Reports on Human Rights Practices*, 721.

Poland

All quotations except 1, 2 & 3 are from Joanna Regulska. 'Women and Power in Poland: Hopes or Reality?', in *Women Transforming Politics*, 179–80, 185 & 186. Quotations 1, 2 & 3 are all from Renata Siemienska. 'Polish Women as the Object and Subject of Politics During and After the Communist Period', in *Women and Politics Worldwide*, 621, 613 & 616.

Sri Lanka

All quotations not attributed in the text are from *Country Reports on Human Rights Practices*, 1392, 1393 & 1394.

Turkey

Quotations here are from Nermin Abadan-Unat and Oya Tokgöz. 'Turkish Women as Agents of Social Change in a Pluralist Democracy', in *Women and Politics Worldwide*, 708, 709 & 716.

United Kingdom of Great Britain and Northern Ireland

Quotations 1 & 2 are from Joyce Gelb. 'Feminism in Britain: Politics without Power?', in *The New Women's Movement*, 103, 116. Quotations 3, 4 & 5 are from Joni Lovenduski. 'The Rules of the Political Game: Feminism and Politics in Great Britain', in *Women and Politics Worldwide*, 305, 300, 308.

Selected Bibliography

Select Bibliography

The following books were particularly helpful in connection with this project.

Bystydzienski, Jill M, ed. *Women Transforming Politics*, Bloomington & Indianapolis: Indiana University Press, 1992.

Dahlerup, Drude, ed. *The New Women's Movement*, London: SAGE Publications, 1986.

Genovese, Michael A, ed. *Women as National Leaders*, Newbury Park, CA: SAGE Publications, 1993.

Iglitzin, Lynne B, & Ruth Ross, eds. *Women in the World: A Comparative Study*, Santa Barbara: Clio Books, 1976.

Iglitzin, Lynne B, & Ruth Ross, eds. *Women in the World, 1975–1985, The Women's Decade*, Santa Barbara: ABC-CLIO, 1986.

Nelson, Barbara J, & Najma Chowdhury, eds. *Women and Politics Worldwide*, New Haven & London: Yale University Press, 1994.

Opfell, Olga S. *Women Prime Ministers and Presidents*, Jefferson, NC: McFarland & Co., 1993. This book deserves special acknowledgment for making available biographical information that is difficult to obtain.

Witt, Linda, Karen M Paget & Glenna Matthews. *Running as a Woman*, New York: The Free Press, 1994. Recommended reading for any woman thinking of entering politics in the United States.

Index